the
chesapeake bay
in maryland · an atlas of natural resources

the
chesapeake bay
in maryland · an atlas of natural resources

edited and illustrated by alice jane lippson for the natural resources institute of the university of maryland

the johns hopkins university press · baltimore and london

Contribution No. 500, Natural Resources Institute,
University of Maryland

The Johns Hopkins University Press, Baltimore, Maryland 21218
The Johns Hopkins University Press Ltd., London

Library of Congress Catalog Card Number 72-12352
ISBN 0-8018-1467-7 (clothbound edition)
ISBN 0-8018-1468-5 (paperback edition)
Manufactured in the United States of America

Originally published, 1973
Johns Hopkins Paperbacks edition, 1973

Library of Congress Cataloging in Publication Data will be
found on the last printed page of this book.

frontispiece photo by John Wilson, Chesapeake Biological
Laboratory

contents

contributors

This book is a compilation of the knowledge and experience of many scientists who have worked on the Chesapeake Bay and studied the various elements that make up the biological system of this significant and interesting body of water.

Those who have contributed to this volume are as follows:

John W. Bishop, *University of Richmond*

Joseph G. Boone, *Maryland Department of Natural Resources*

W. R. Carter III, *Maryland Department of Natural Resources*

James F. Casey IV, *Maryland Department of Natural Resources*

L. Eugene Cronin, *Chesapeake Biological Laboratory*

William B. Cronin, *Chesapeake Bay Institute*

William L. Dovel, formerly at *Chesapeake Biological Laboratory,* now at *Boyce Thompson Institute of Plant Research, Inc.*

Elgin A. Dunnington, *Chesapeake Biological Laboratory*

David A. Flemer, *Chesapeake Biological Laboratory*

Frank L. Hamons, *Maryland Department of Natural Resources*

Donald R. Heinle, *Chesapeake Biological Laboratory*

Howard J. King, *Maryland Department of Natural Resources*

Ted S. Y. Koo, *Chesapeake Biological Laboratory*

Alice J. Lippson, formerly at *Chesapeake Biological Laboratory,* now at *Martin Marietta Corporate Research and Development Laboratory / RIAS*

Robert L. Lippson, formerly at *Chesapeake Biological Laboratory,* now with *National Marine Fisheries Service, Oxford Laboratory*

Hayes T. Pfitzenmeyer, *Chesapeake Biological Laboratory*

Donald W. Pritchard, *Chesapeake Bay Institute*

Charles K. Rawls, *Chesapeake Biological Laboratory*

Douglas E. Ritchie, Jr., *Chesapeake Biological Laboratory*

J. Albert Sherk, Jr., *Chesapeake Biological Laboratory*

John H. Steenis, *Bureau of Sport Fisheries and Wildlife, Patuxent Wildlife Research Center*

Robert E. Stewart, *Bureau of Sport Fisheries and Wildlife, Northern Prairie Wildlife Research Center*

Vernon D. Stotts, *Maryland Department of Natural Resources*

Martin L. Wiley, *Chesapeake Biological Laboratory*

The initials of the contributor or contributors for each section and map are listed at the end of the appropriate article. The addresses of the various institutes and organizations are as follows:

Chesapeake Biological Laboratory, Natural Resources Institute, University of Maryland, Solomons, Maryland

Chesapeake Bay Institute, The Johns Hopkins University, Baltimore, Maryland

Maryland Department of Natural Resources, Annapolis, Maryland

National Marine Fisheries Service, Oxford Laboratory, Oxford, Maryland

Bureau of Sport Fisheries and Wildlife, Northern Prairie Wildlife Research Center, Jamestown, North Dakota

Bureau of Sport Fisheries and Wildlife, Patuxent Wildlife Research Center, Laurel, Maryland

Boyce Thompson Institute of Plant Research, Inc., Yonkers, New York

University of Richmond, Richmond, Virginia

Martin Marietta Corporate Research and Development Laboratory/RIAS, Baltimore, Maryland

foreword

Maryland contains within its borders the low-salinity half of a large estuary, from fifteen to twenty sub-estuaries at the mouths of rivers, several major sounds and bays, and hundreds of tidal estuarine creeks and small harbors. This extensive region, with its salinity between 0 and 20 parts of salt per 1,000 parts of water, is unique among the United States and unusual in the world. It possesses distinctive characteristics which contribute to its high human value. It receives all the benefits and burdens that flow from two great interstate rivers, the Potomac and the Susquehanna, and from many others—the Choptank, Chester, Patuxent, Nanticoke, and a host of smaller systems. While these bring sediments and some pollutants, they also provide nutrient chemicals and an average flow of about 58,000 cubic feet per second of fresh water, which maintains the salinity pattern. This run-off is not stable, however, but comes in high flows of late winter and spring, and low flows of late summer and fall—with sufficient variation to make each year different.

The result is a biological treasure. The nutrients make it possible for plankton and rooted aquatic plants to produce enormous quantities of organic material. These feed the world's largest crops of oysters and clams in water salty enough for them but not salty enough for their worst natural predators. The estuarine waters of Maryland also support large populations of many species of fish, and the vital low-salinity region, where salt content is between 0 and 10 parts of salt per 1,000 parts of water, is the required habitat for an almost invisible resource, the eggs and larvae of rock, shad, herring, and many other species which spawn in the rivers, bay, and ocean. This is the most important spawning and nursery area in the world for the rock or striped bass, and it is of extraordinary importance for other species, as will be shown in subsequent summaries.

Man has imposed many changes on the Chesapeake Bay, and especially on its tributaries. Baltimore and Washington, at the head of navigable water in two separate tributaries, contribute wastes, silt, exotic chemicals, and the demand for dredged channels and for fisheries and recreation. Many smaller communities also add their impact. The quantities of treated sewage, of wasted heat from power plants, of solid wastes from communities, and of chemical additions to the estuary are now so great that exceptional care must be taken to make and use an accurate prediction of their effects.

Rather suddenly, in perhaps thirty years, it has become obvious that various uses of the Bay are beginning to conflict. Dredge spoil to improve shipping threatens oyster beds and fish nursery areas. Release of waste chemicals and heat often disturbs the ecosystem. Industrial sites may be located too close to essential spawning grounds. Diversion of water for the benefit of some people may reduce the income or quality of life for others. Future uses of the Bay must be planned on a better basis of knowledge and a better concept of careful balance and protection of desired objectives than have prevailed in the past. The State of Maryland recognized this need by appointing a Chesapeake Bay Interagency Planning Committee, which was charged with accumulating available information on present uses of the Maryland portion of the Bay and with developing the basis for wise planning for the future.

When the Committee sought a summary of the aquatic resources of Maryland, it became painfully clear that no such summary had yet been made. Certain portions (oyster-bar distribution, wetlands charts, etc.) had been drawn and were highly useful, but it was not possible to discern which species might be affected at specific sites. The information needed to locate quickly the areas valuable as nurseries, migration paths, shellfish beds, or for other functions has existed only in the experienced judgment of a small number of people.

We decided to bring together as much of this information as possible, I sugested that a series of resource maps be assembled, and thus this atlas was developed. A large number of scientists and resource managers have contributed brief but expert summaries of data and knowledge. These have been edited into a consistent format by Mrs. Alice Jane Lippson (formerly Mansueti), and she has added unique contributions. Mrs. Lippson was the Scientific Illustrator at the Chesapeake Biological Laboratory from 1954 until 1971. She has developed the ability to design and create excellent and highly informative visual summaries of complex information, and that skill is richly evident in the following pages. Only she could have brought together, illustrated, edited, and produced this atlas.

This is, however, only a beginning. Maryland and Virginia scientists will expand the cooperation in research which has existed for many years, so that the entire Bay, as well as its local parts, can be better understood. We plan to accumulate additional details about the rich biological treasures of the Bay and to publish them in other, more specific, atlases. Future efforts must include the exact mapping of resources of the whole Bay system. Each portion of the Bay, each tributary, each cove, and each creek has its own patterns and role in the ecosystem of the Bay region, and knowledge of such details will be of increasing importance as increasing numbers of people use this great estuary for a host of purposes.

L. EUGENE CRONIN
Director
Chesapeake Biological Laboratory
Natural Resources Institute
University of Maryland

preface

This atlas is a collection of maps that describe the distribution of the resources of Maryland's portion of the Chesapeake Bay. Hopefully, it will be of interest to many people: the layman who would like to know more about the biology and dynamics of the Chesapeake Bay, the teacher, the conservationist or resource planner, and the scientist, who will find it a useful general reference.

The maps and their accompanying texts have been treated as separate chapters and are authored by different individuals or a number of individuals. Because of this, the style of writing and the kinds of information presented vary somewhat.

Maryland's portion of Chesapeake Bay includes the upper Bay and all its tributaries, from the Virginia state line north to the Susquehanna River. The state line on the Potomac River runs along the Virginia shore and excludes the many streams and creeks that empty into the Potomac from the Virginia side. In many instances, these Virginia tributaries have been included within the scope of the mapping. These exceptions were made because the particular pattern of distribution up the Potomac would appear erroneous if cut straight along the borderline. Another exception has been made in the case of Chincoteague Bay along the ocean coast of Maryland. Originally, there was no intention to include this body of water. However, in a few cases, this area was mapped by the contributor, and so it was retained as additional useful information.

The Chesapeake Bay is a dynamic environment with many internal cycles and pulses that vary from night to day, from season to season, and from year to year. The Bay's physical properties—its temperature, its salinity, its turbidity, and so on—all reflect these alternations. Likewise, Bay animal and plant populations undergo regular fluctuations. Most of these cycles are normal and predictable, but very often conditions arise that cause long-term or permanent changes. Consequently, what is correct today in our assessment of Bay life may radically change in the future.

The maps should be read with a number of points in mind. In most instances, general distribution is shown. In the case of highly motile species —fish and crabs, for instance—the pattern shows where the species can be expected at the particular season indicated. This does not mean, however, that the species in question will necessarily be found everywhere within the plotted area during that season. Even non-migrating species, such as oysters or rooted aquatic plants, are susceptible to great variability in their distribution.

The scale of the maps does not allow detailed inclusion of each small tributary, creek, or stream.

The lines of demarcation of the areas on the maps should not be considered impassable walls across the water. There is always a gradient zone of distributional limits. Changing conditions may reduce or increase the general range of animal or plant species. Likewise, the physical parameters as drawn on the introductory maps will shift and change and in turn affect the distribution of species.

The maps consider only the normal distribution of species. The occasional records of stragglers outside these areas have not been taken into account.

The choice of what to include in this collection of maps was based on a number of factors: whether the species was important to man either recreationally or commercially; whether the species was important in the ecosystem as a food source for other animals; whether it was an important physical parameter which directly affects life in the Bay; and/or whether there were sufficient data available for mapping.

The kind of information available was important in mapping distributions. The greater the amount of data available, the more detailed and accurate are the maps. In some cases, only certain parts of the Bay are mapped, either because the data were totally unavailable or because the kinds of data available (sometimes a great amount of factual material) were not analyzed in a manner which could be transferred to a map. This was particularly true of such matters as the distribution of chlorophyll a, or the distribution of sediments in the tributaries. Most maps include a statement concerning the adequacy of the data.

The contributors' initials are listed at the end of each section. The first of these persons contributed the original material; the others contributed additional information, which often was of a very substantial nature.

The literature cited only partially indicates the sources for mapping. Much of the information has come from the personal knowledge and experience of the authors and reflects the years of field studies and research projects conducted by the institutes and organizations that have worked in the Bay.

In a book of this nature, it was necessary to rely on many people. The atlas would not have been possible without the willingness of all the contributors to share their knowledge. In addition, I would like to make special acknowledgments: first of all to my husband, Robert L. Lippson, who has been my prime source of encouragement, and to whom I turned for help in all the many questions and problems that arose; to Pat Pauley, who labored industriously over the many overlays necessary for the printer; to Lee Parks, for typing the manuscript; to Dr. L. Eugene Cronin, not only for giving the project the support of the Natural Resources Institute, but also for his personal interest and help throughout and for his final careful editing; to William Bergoffen of the Natural Resources Institute, for his editorial suggestions; to Ann Szymkowitz, for her drawings of the blue crab and the oyster; to Don Lear and his staff at the Environmental Protection Agency, Annapolis, Maryland; to Roy Metzgar of the Maryland Department of State Planning; to Michael Cook of the Publications Office of the University of Maryland, for his knowledgeable assistance in the final production of the atlas; and to Helen Lang, librarian of the Oxford Laboratory of the National Marine Fisheries Service.

ALICE JANE LIPPSON

the
chesapeake bay
in maryland · an atlas of natural resources

the chesapeake bay

The Chesapeake Bay is the largest estuary in the United States and one of the most useful in the world. It was created during the last 15,000 years by the flooding of the lower valley of the greatest river on the East Coast, the mighty Susquehanna. As a drowned valley, it has hundreds of peripheral rivers, bays, and creeks, a very long shoreline, and extensive areas of shallow water. It is about 180 miles long (155 nautical miles), 5–30 miles wide (8–48 kilometers), and up to 175 feet (53 meters) deep. The average depth of the open Bay is 27.6 feet (8.4 meters), and the average depth of the total system, including tributaries, is 21.2 feet (6.5 meters). If all of the water were drained, the ancient channel of the Susquehanna would still be visible, the extensive shallow shoulders would be clearly outlined, and the massive quantities of soft sediment which are slowly filling the Bay and all of its tributaries would be apparent.

The open Bay has a surface area of about 2,500 square miles (6,500 square kilometers), and the total estuarine system, including tributaries, has an area of about 4,400 square miles (11,500 square kilometers). The low-tide volume of the Bay is about 13.7 trillion gallons (52 billion cubic meters), and that of the whole system is about 19.6 trillion gallons (74 billion cubic meters or 11.6 cubic miles). The total shoreline of the Bay and its tributaries is estimated to be 8,100 miles (13,033 kilometers), with 4,000 miles (6,400 kilometers) in Maryland and 4,100 miles (6,600 kilometers) in Virginia.

The Maryland portion includes those parts of the Bay and its tributaries which lie north of Smith Point, at the entrance to the Potomac River. The state owns the Potomac, but not its southern tributaries (since the interstate boundary crosses from headland to headland) nor the portion in the District of Columbia. The Maryland-Virginia line runs across the Bay from the mouth of the Potomac through the middle of Pocomoke Sound on the Eastern Shore. Therefore, the Maryland portion includes the deepest hole in the Bay (at Bloody Point, at the south end of Kent Island) and the narrowest segment (between Kent Island and Sandy Point), while the widest region, at the Virginia line, is shared by both states.

The present population of the total Chesapeake Bay watershed of 74,000 square miles is about 8 million, and it may increase to 10–12 million by the year 2000. In Maryland and the District of Columbia, approximately 2,313,000 persons live within twenty miles of the Bay and its tributaries, and most of them affect and are affected by it. They cluster in the urban and suburban centers around Baltimore and Washington, major foci in the emerging eastern megalopolis from Boston to Norfolk. Many, however, live along the shore in the hundreds of small cities, towns, and villages that arose because of the presence of the Bay. The living and quality of life of the residents of these communities are inextricably tied to the Bay and its rivers.

L. E. C.

Sources: Cronin, W. B. (1971); Cronin, L. E. (1967).

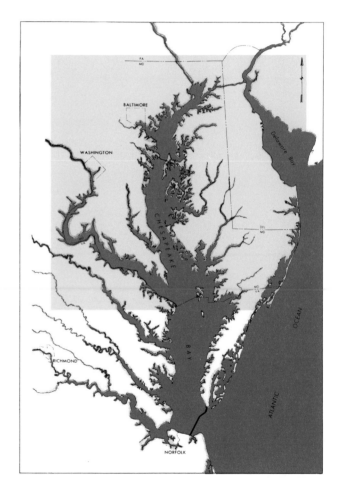

The Chesapeake Bay in its entirety. The shaded square indicates the area encompassed by the distributional maps of this atlas.

chesapeake bay
in maryland

PLACE NAMES

depths, tides, and currents

Physical features must be considered for a full understanding of the biological aspects of Chesapeake Bay. Depths, tides, currents, salinity, sedimentary deposits, and temperature are some of the most important of these physical factors. One or a combination of a number of these will directly affect or control the distribution of a species within the Bay system.

Depths

The Chesapeake Bay is a comparatively shallow body of water, generally low-lying and marshy in many areas. The depth of the Bay varies from a few spots 130–170 feet (40–52 meters) deep to the tidal marshes exposed at low tide and located up the tributaries. Shallow shoulders, less than 30 feet deep, line the edges of the Bay and all tributaries, providing a favorable habitat for shellfish and many fishes. The deeper channels lie along the eastern side of the Bay, and the saltier water from the ocean moves up the Bay in these channels and maintains the salt balance of the Bay. The head and the mouth of the Bay have more shoals and are the areas where dredging is conducted to create and maintain the deeper channels required by large ships.

The largest artificial channels in Maryland include the channels and approaches to Baltimore Harbor and the artificial Chesapeake and Delaware Canal, which connects the Elk River to Delaware Bay. That canal was first dug in the early nineteenth century as a private venture. It is now 35 feet deep, has a minimum width of 450 feet, and carries more traffic than the Panama Canal.

Tides

The surface of the Bay slopes slightly from the headwaters to the Atlantic Ocean, thus maintaining a net flow toward the sea. The slope is not obvious, partly because it is very gradual, but it is vastly overshadowed by the diurnal tides, which move up the Bay from the ocean twice in each 24.8 hours. Each tide (the level of the water, *not* the tidal currents) moves up the Bay in about 13 hours, so that a high tide at the mouth moves up the Bay in a progressive wave and changes to a standing wave, which reaches its highest range at just about the same time that the following tidal high begins at the Capes.

The tidal range is greatest at the mouth of the Bay (2.5 feet, 0.76 meters) and at the end of most

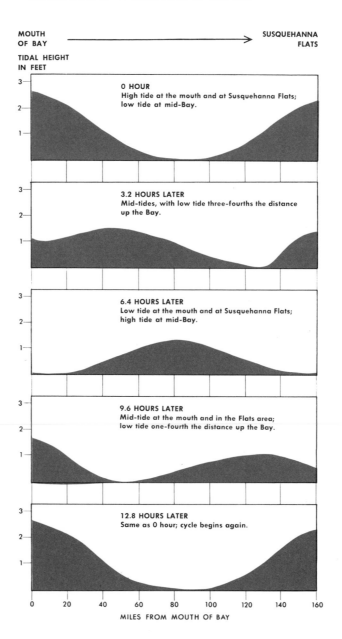

PROGRESSION OF A TIDAL HIGH UP THE BAY

MOUTH OF BAY → SUSQUEHANNA FLATS

TIDAL HEIGHT IN FEET

0 HOUR
High tide at the mouth and at Susquehanna Flats; low tide at mid-Bay.

3.2 HOURS LATER
Mid-tides, with low tide three-fourths the distance up the Bay.

6.4 HOURS LATER
Low tide at the mouth and at Susquehanna Flats; high tide at mid-Bay.

9.6 HOURS LATER
Mid-tide at the mouth and in the Flats area; low tide one-fourth the distance up the Bay.

12.8 HOURS LATER
Same as 0 hour; cycle begins again.

MILES FROM MOUTH OF BAY

of the large rivers, and is about 2 feet (0.61 meters) at the head of the Bay. Much of Maryland has a tidal range of 1–2 feet.

Currents

Tidal currents are the horizontal movements caused by changes in the elevation of the surface through tidal changes. The Bay currents are usually very moderate and average well below 0.5 knots (0.9 kilometers per hour), except in the upper Bay

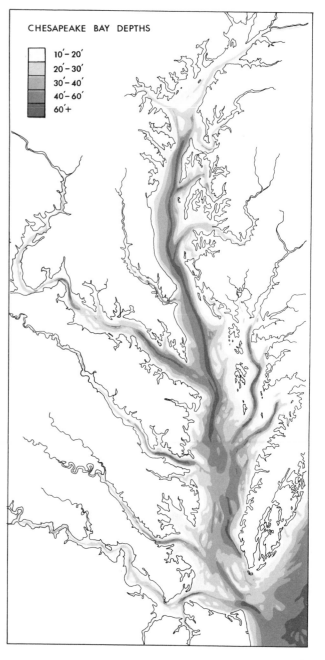

CHESAPEAKE BAY DEPTHS

10'– 20'
20'– 30'
30'– 40'
40'– 60'
60'+

or in bottlenecks, where they may reach as high as 1.5 knots (2.8 kilometers per hour) during the ebb tide. It should be stressed that the predicted tidal ranges and currents are derived from long-term averages. Local weather conditions, particularly wind effects, may cause "tidal" ranges and currents to range several times above or below their normal level.

W. B. C.

Source: U.S. Department of Commerce, Coast and Geodetic Survey (1930).

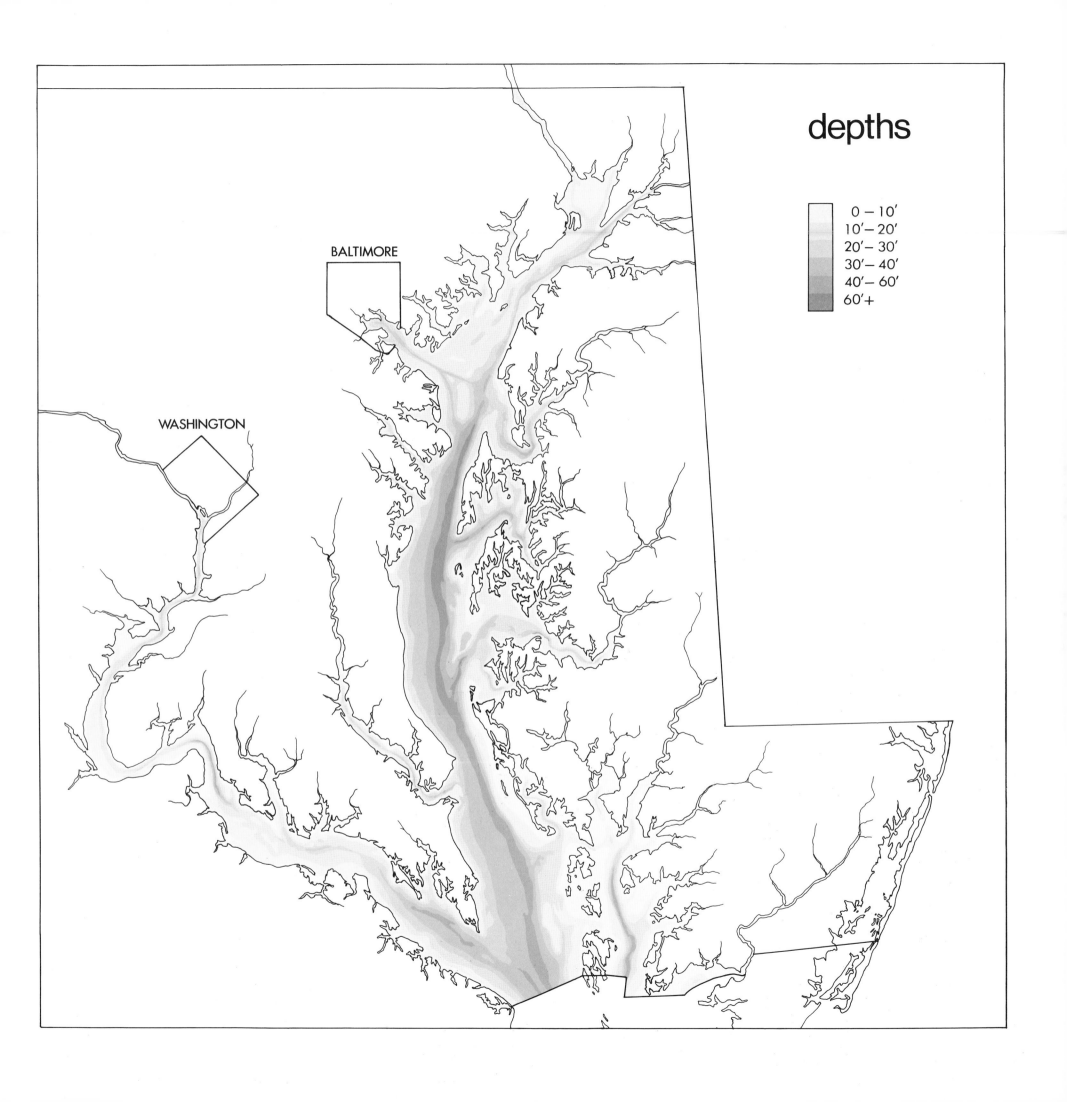

depths

0 – 10'
10' – 20'
20' – 30'
30' – 40'
40' – 60'
60'+

BALTIMORE

WASHINGTON

salinity

The salt content (or salinity) of the water throughout Chesapeake Bay and its tributaries is an important physical factor which affects the distributional patterns of animal and plant species, whose adaptation to any area is regulated by the amount of salinity they can tolerate. From the site of freshwater inflow of the Susquehanna River at the head of the Bay, the salt content increases in a more or less regular manner along the length of the Bay, reaching a salinity of nearly full sea water at the mouth. Characteristically, salinity also increases with depth. In any one area, the vertical variation in salinity shows an upper layer of very slow increase with depth, an intermediate layer of more rapid increase, and a deep layer in which, again, the salinity increase with depth is small. The salt content also varies across the Bay, from lower salinities on the western side of the Bay to higher salinities along the Eastern Shore. Although the greater runoff of fresh water from the western shore contributes to this lateral difference, the major cause of this variation involves the influence of the earth's rotation.

The maps show the characteristic features of horizontal salinity distribution for spring and autumn. Salinity is defined as the number of parts of salt per 1,000 parts of water. A line drawn to delineate the extension of a salinity value is called an isohaline line. Isohalines are drawn for each whole number increase from 0 to 29 parts per thousand (designated o/oo). The Chesapeake Bay in Maryland rarely has a salinity greater than 20 o/oo, which makes this area a true estuarine environment, where the runoff of fresh water mixing with incoming ocean waters results in a gradient of intermediate salinities.

Minimum salinities occur in the spring, when essentially fresh water extends, on the average, to Pooles Island; maximum salinities occur in the autumn, when low but measurable ocean-derived salt concentrations extend onto the Susquehanna Flats.

The intensity of the vertical variation in salinity also changes seasonally, with the largest vertical gradient occurring in the spring and the weakest vertical gradient occurring in the autumn. The vertical pattern is, however, highly variable in time and space within any season, depending to a large extent on recent local weather.

This summary is based on the extensive surveys of Chesapeake Bay and its tributaries conducted by the Chesapeake Bay Institute of The Johns Hopkins University between July 1949 and January 1951. The extent of these surveys and the detailed analysis which has been made of resulting data provide excellent bases for summaries. The facing maps show average salinity conditions. Actual salinity readings will vary considerably (see upper Bay detail map).

D. W. P.

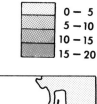

	0 – 5
	5 – 10
	10 – 15
	15 – 20

Detail of surface salinity of the upper Chesapeake Bay on specific dates (*Spring,* April 24–May 1, 1964; *Autumn,* November 9–13, 1964) showing how actual figures can differ substantially from the averages. Surface salinity in parts per thousand.

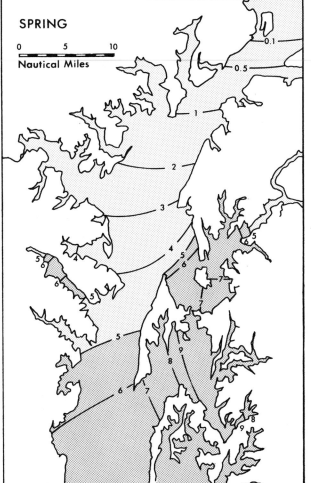

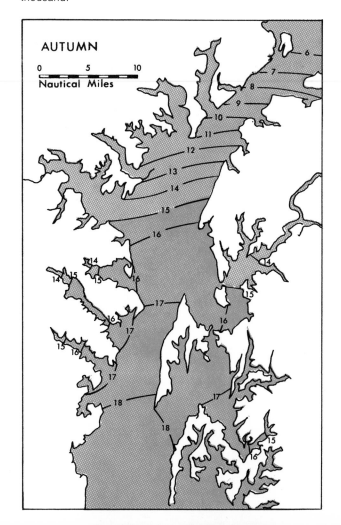

Sources: Pritchard (1952, 1966); Whaley and Hopkins (1952).

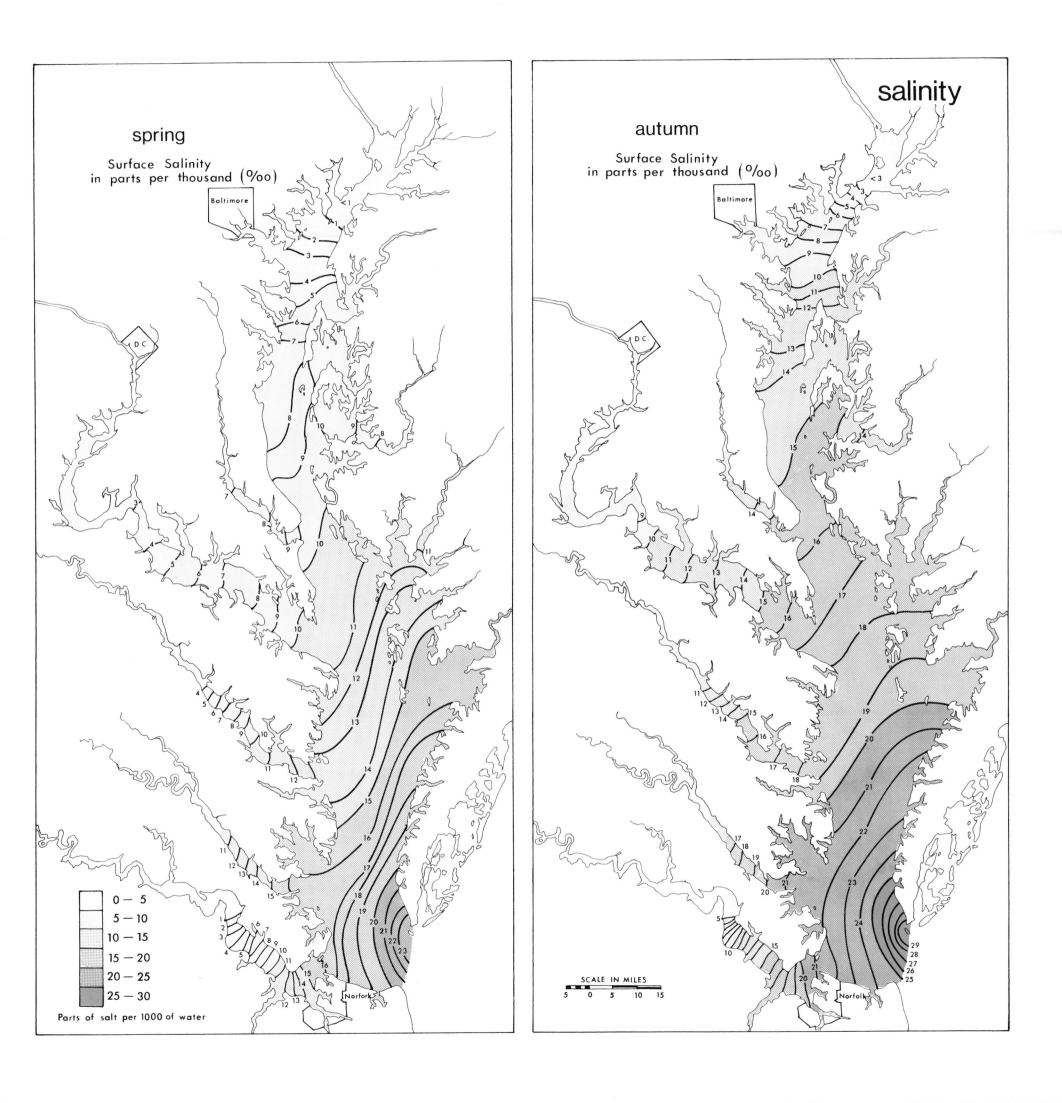

spring

Surface Salinity
in parts per thousand (⁰/oo)

salinity

autumn

Surface Salinity
in parts per thousand (⁰/oo)

	0 – 5
	5 – 10
	10 – 15
	15 – 20
	20 – 25
	25 – 30

Parts of salt per 1000 of water

SCALE IN MILES
5 0 5 10 15

sediments

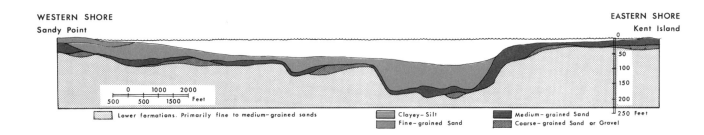

WESTERN SHORE
Sandy Point

EASTERN SHORE
Kent Island

Lower formations. Primarily fine to medium-grained sands   Clayey-Silt   Medium-grained Sand
Fine-grained Sand   Coarse-grained Sand or Gravel

Cross section of sediment layers in the area of the Chesapeake Bay bridge (see map). In this area of the Bay, coarse sand and gravel layers are covered by other relatively thin layers of finer sediments. Note that the vertical scale is only one-tenth the measure of the horizontal scale. The Bay is so relatively shallow that it would be impossible to illustrate this section graphically using equal scales.

The sedimentary structure of the bottom in any area of the Chesapeake Bay or its tributaries limits the species of plant and animal life that occur there. Benthic, or bottom-dwelling, animals and rooted aquatic plants tolerate specific kinds of bottom materials. Benthic populations in estuaries usually thrive best in areas of medium- to fine-grained sand. Comparatively few bottom species live in the clayey silt of channel areas.

Sediments are continually added to the Bay from the washing of soil into the tributaries and from the erosion of the banks and shores. Surface land erosion is greatest during periods of high rainfall and river flow, and most shore erosion occurs during storms. The sediments introduced are slowly filling the tributaries and even the Bay itself.

The muddiest waters of the Bay are usually found between Tolchester and the mouth of the Sassafras River. Silt from the Susquehanna tends to settle there, but tidal currents and occasional winds resuspend the particles again and again. Sediments provide an enormous surface area for the absorption of large quantities of the various elements and compounds which are deposited on the floor of the Bay along with the sediments.

Homogeneous gray or black mud forms the floor of the main channel of Chesapeake Bay and of the sloping bottom west of this channel. These areas include the deepest parts of the ancient Susquehanna Valley and have the greatest sediment accumulation. Channel mud is composed primarily of silt-sized particles and varying amounts of clay and water. The sand content of this mud is highest near the mouth of the Bay. Mud distribution in the Bay proper is asymmetrical because of the asymmetric bottom topography. Mud also forms the channel bottoms in the Bay's Coastal Plain tributaries.

Western shore sands tend to be well sorted and are coarse- to fine-grained. Particle size decreases between the shoreline (the source of these sands) and the zone of bottom mud (the channel). Some Western shore sands form a series of terraces which extend outward from Calvert Cliffs. These sands are medium- to coarse-grained.

Eastern Shore near-channel sands vary greatly in grain size. In some areas, the median diameter of particles increases away from the shoreline. Eastern Shore drowned-flats sands occur on broad, flat, shallow portions of the Bay near Tangier and Pocomoke Sounds. Tidal currents are split by the flats and travel around them. These sand particles are fine- to medium-grained, are well sorted, and are nearly all the same size.

Cores taken in channel areas typically exhibit an upper black layer of clay which grades downward into a soft, gray layer. The black layer is usually thickest in the channel of the mid-Bay area, gradually decreases outside the channel area, and may be absent in shallow water. However, this black layer is seldom very thick.

Sediments in the northern Bay, Tangier Sound, and Pocomoke Sound exhibit alternating bands of black and gray or brownish-gray mud which vary in thickness. Such differences in the color of sediments may be caused by differences in organic content, with lighter-colored sediments containing less organic material than darker ones.

Black, highly carbonaceous muds may form an environment which is toxic to benthic life. Anaerobic conditions and the formation of toxic hydrogen sulfide can occur where the circulation of overlying water is blocked. Such extremely poor benthic conditions, coupled with the dark, soft character of the channel muds, may account for the absence of important benthic species in channel areas of the Bay.

Even though most of the floor of the Bay has been examined, much research remains to be done on the geological history of the Bay and on sedimentary conditions and processes.

The results of sediment-sampling programs that have been conducted in various Bay tributaries are not presently available in a form which can be transferred to a map. Consequently, only sediments of the Bay proper are drawn on the accompanying map.

J. A. S.

Sources: Ryan (1953); Biggs (1970).

Illustration of the resuspension of bottom sediments by storm waves. Sediment sampling was conducted in the area of the upper Chesapeake Bay between Turkey Point and Tolchester on May 5–6, 1966. From May 6 to May 12 a storm occurred with very high winds. The sediment picture at the end of this storm, graphed from samples taken on May 11–12, shows the great amount of resuspension of sediments that can be caused by storm waves.

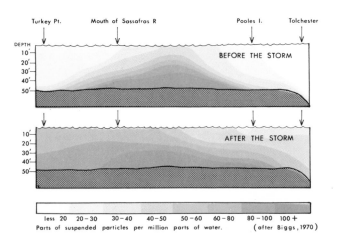

Turkey Pt.   Mouth of Sassafras R   Pooles I.   Tolchester

BEFORE THE STORM

AFTER THE STORM

less 20   20–30   30–40   40–50   50–60   60–80   80–100   100+
Parts of suspended particles per million parts of water.   (after Biggs, 1970)

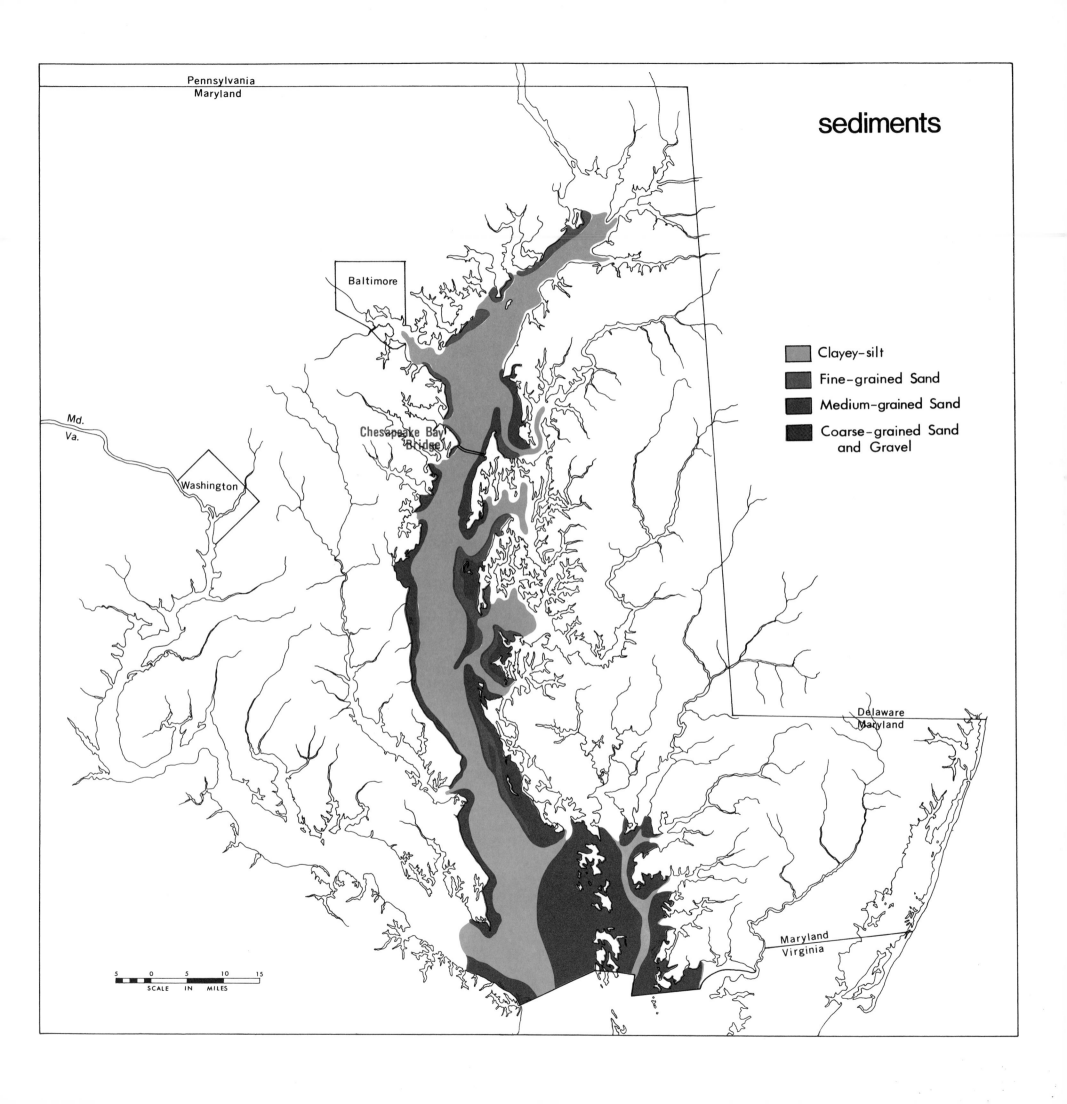

sediments

Pennsylvania
Maryland

Baltimore

Md.
Va.

Washington

Chesapeake Bay
Bridge

Delaware
Maryland

Maryland
Virginia

Clayey-silt

Fine-grained Sand

Medium-grained Sand

Coarse-grained Sand
and Gravel

5   0   5   10   15
SCALE   IN   MILES

marshes

There are many marshes along the shores of Chesapeake Bay and along the edges of its tributaries, creeks, and inlets. The many kinds of plants which make up these marshes are dependent on the presence of water above ground level at least some of the time. This special kind of vegetation gives marshes a character which is totally different from that of dry land. Marshes are vital to the ecology of the Bay system, for, not only do they supply cover and food for many species of waterfowl, songbirds, mammals, fishes, crabs, and many other aquatic animals, but, as they decompose, they return important nutrients to the entire water system. Because of dredging, filling, and other alterations, however, many of Maryland's 214,000 acres of Bay marshes have been lost.

Marshlands in the Chesapeake Bay region vary in their make-up and appearance according to factors such as salinity, tidal fluctuations, depth of inundating water, and type of dominant vegetation. Accordingly, marshes are here separated into five types. Within each type, only some of the dominant plant species are discussed. Many other species also will be found in each area. Marsh plants are distinguished from rooted aquatic plants in that they are emergent plants and are above water level at least part of the time. Many rooted aquatic plants, particularly widgeongrass and sago pondweed, are an integral part of the marshes, but their origin is below the low-tide level.

Estuarine River Marshes have developed wherever tidewaters extend inland along the narrowed valley floors of tributary streams. River marshes are scattered throughout Maryland's Chesapeake region. The largest, along the Nanticoke River, is in some places as wide as two miles. Other large marshes of this type occur in most of the larger tributaries. Small marshes are found along the numerous small tidal streams, including those of Chincoteague Bay.

River marshes are divided into two types: freshwater estuarine river marshes upstream and brackish-water estuarine river marshes downstream.

Fresh-water estuarine river marshes, found at the upper reaches of tributaries, occur in fresh-to-very-slightly-brackish water. Tidal fluctuations are especially pronounced in this type of marsh. A wide variety of marsh plants occurs, and species tend to be distributed according to water depth. Of the many species found here, the most common are: *pickerelweed and yellow waterlily,* which occur in deeper portions near open water; *river bulrush, rosemallow, and phragmites,* which grow in shallow marginal areas; and *wildrice,* which dominates sectors of intermediate depth.

Brackish-water estuarine river marshes are located farther downstream in waters of greater salinity. These marshes include a wide variety of plants. Among the important species are: *big cordgrass,* which occurs in nearly all areas, including those which are intermediate between fresh and brackish marshes; *narrowleaf cattail and olney three-square,* which are found interspersed in stands of big cordgrass; and *rosemallow and phragmites,* which grow in shallow marginal areas.

Fresh Estuarine Bay Marshes have developed on broad, shallow estuarine flats that are flooded by fresh or slightly brackish tidewaters. Tidal streams of the drainage system usually are broad, poorly defined, and often merge into numerous large connecting ponds. As shown on the map, there are two major areas where this type of marsh occurs: one in the upper Bay between Baltimore and the Susquehanna Flats; the other on the Eastern Shore, in Dorchester County. Major species include: *olney three-square,* which is spread over extensive areas, particularly in the broad zones closest to drainage channels; *narrowleaf cattail,* which grows in areas where the water level is more stable, in headwaters, and in areas protected by narrow barrier beaches; *common three-square,* which occurs in marsh meadows in shallow areas along the edges of the marsh; *dwarf spikerush,* which is found in the mudbare, shallow flats often exposed at low tide; and *white waterlily,* which grows densely in ponds and creeks, where the water level is relatively stable.

Brackish Estuarine Bay Marshes occur in areas characterized by a complex mosaic of ponds, creeks, and marshes. Much of the great marsh area in Dorchester County is of this type. The dominant plant species in different areas are: *big cordgrass,* which grows in the narrow zone along the margins of tidal creeks and ponds; *hightide bush,* which is found in high, marginal areas of marsh; *saltmeadow cordgrass,* which occurs in the marsh meadows of well-drained zones near creeks and ponds and is adjacent to narrow borders of big cordgrass; *saltmarsh cordgrass,* which grows with saltmeadow cordgrass or replaces it, sometimes on well-drained tidal flats; *olney three-square,* which is found in extensive, poorly drained, shallow depressions normally covered with surface water; and *saltgrass,* which is commonly associated with olney three-square and saltmarsh cordgrass.

Salt Estuarine Bay Marshes occur in lower Maryland Bay waters, where salinity is relatively high and tidal fluctuations are narrow. Species include: *saltmeadow cordgrass,* which is found in large meadows in better-drained areas above the normal high-tide mark; *saltmarsh cordgrass,* which occurs along tidal streams in narrow, well-drained zones and is frequently inundated; *saltmarsh bulrush* and *saltgrass,* which grow in patches in poorly drained, depressed areas; and *hightide bush,* which forms narrow strips on ridges of high ground, along the upper portions of tidal streams.

Coastal Embayed Marshes fringe the Chincoteague Bay. In these marshes, saltmarsh cordgrass predominates, growing in nearly pure stands throughout most of the area. Other common species, growing in scattered patches, include saltmeadow cordgrass, saltgrass, and hightide bush.

This classification of marshland types was originally proposed in reference to waterfowl habitats. It is based on an extensive sampling of plants in each area, so that Maryland marshes are now recorded with fairly good accuracy.

R. E. S.

Sources: Metzgar (1972); Stewart (1962).

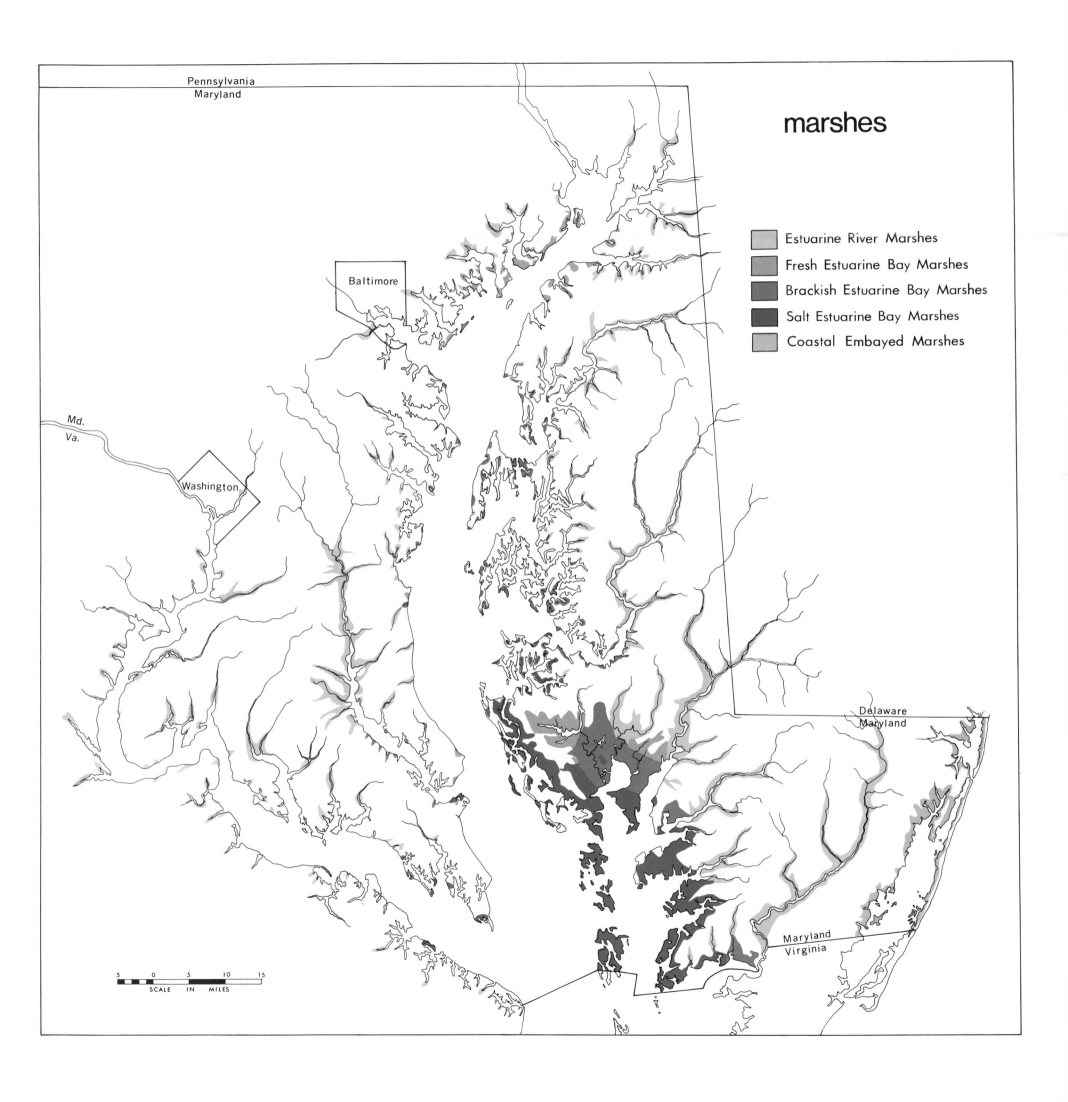

marshes

Estuarine River Marshes
Fresh Estuarine Bay Marshes
Brackish Estuarine Bay Marshes
Salt Estuarine Bay Marshes
Coastal Embayed Marshes

Pennsylvania
Maryland

Baltimore

Md.
Va.

Washington

Delaware
Maryland

Maryland
Virginia

5   0   5   10   15
SCALE IN MILES

rooted aquatic plants

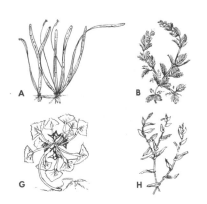  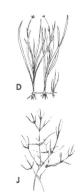  

COMMON ROOTED AQUATIC PLANTS OF MARYLAND

A. Wildcelery—*Vallisneria americana*
B. Milfoil, Eurasian Watermilfoil—*Myriophyllum spicatum*
C. Waterweed—*Elodea canadensis*
D. Mud Plantain, Waterstargrass—*Heteranthera dubia*
E. Southern Naiad, Bushy Pondweed—*Najas Guadalupensis*
F. Sago Pondweed—*Potamogeton pectinatus*
G. Waterchestnut—*Trapa natans*
H. Redheadgrass—*Potamogeton perfoliatus*
I. Widgeongrass—*Ruppia maritima*
J. Horned Pondweed—*Zannichellia palustris*
K. Coontail—*Ceratophyllum demersum*
L. Eelgrass—*Zostera marina*

Rooted aquatic plants, like marsh plants, are important food sources for both aquatic animals and waterfowl. Rooted aquatic plants, for the purposes of this atlas and to distinguish them from marsh plants, are those seed-bearing species which are rooted to the bottom and whose leaves usually appear below or just at the surface of the water. The very common sea lettuce, *Ulva lactuca,* appears to be a rooted aquatic plant growing in extensive beds, but it is actually an algal plant. Rooted aquatics are found primarily in the vicinity of open water shoals and shorelines of the Bay in waters shallow enough to allow the plants to reach the surface. Some of the predominant species are found in marsh or wetland ponds or in small guts, but seldom where such areas are subject to frequent drying. The map shows the major areas in which these plants can be expected. The key indicates which plants will ordinarily be found in each area, but plant distribution can be quite variable. Most of the species mentioned here are evident from late spring to early fall.

Plant distribution and abundance are affected by salinity, turbidity, wind and wave action, temperatures, eutrophication, and encroachment by other vegetation. Distribution and abundance patterns often change radically from one season to the next and even within the same growing season.

Information for plotting the distribution of rooted aquatics has been compiled from knowledge obtained from cooperative surveys made by scientists from universities and state and federal agencies, primarily empirical observations from land, water, and air. These observations were made in 1967, 1969, and 1970. To maintain accurate, up-to-date maps, at least three annual surveys of the entire area would have to be made, but at present this is not economically feasible. The distribution of aquatic plants in the upper reaches of Eastern Shore rivers is not mapped here. There is some spotty distribution in these areas in association with the river marshes. Species H. and I. occur in more brackish areas; C. and A. occur in fresher portions. Studies of vegetation in certain Virginia tributaries of the Potomac have been limited.

C. K. R., J. H. S., V. D. S.

Source: Stewart (1962).

AREAS NUMBERED ON THE MAP

CHESAPEAKE BAY

1. Susquehanna R.
2. Susquehanna Flats
3. Northeast R.
4. Elk R., Bohemia R.
5. Sassafras R.
6. Still Pond Cr.
7. Worton Cr., Fairlee Cr.
8. Bush R.
9. Gunpowder R., Bird R., Middle R.
10. Back R., Patapsco R.
11. Magothy R.
12. Severn R.
13. South R.

14. Rhodes R., West R.
15. Chester R.
16. Eastern Neck Is.
17. Eastern Bay
18. Choptank R.
19. Little Choptank R.
20. Patuxent R.
21. Taylor Is.
22. Hooper Is.
23. Honga R., Fishing Bay
24. Nanticoke R., Wicomico R.
25. Tangier Sound and adjacent tributaries
26. Pocomoke Sound

POTOMAC RIVER

I. Matawoman Cr.
II. Nanjemoy Cr.
III. Port Tobacco R.
IV. Piccowaxan Cr.
V. Cuckold Cr.
VI. Cobb Is., Neale Sound
VII. Wicomico R.
VIII. St. Catherine Sound
IX. St. Patrick Cr., Blakiston Is.
X. Colonial Beach
XI. Nomini Bay
XII. Lower Machodoc Cr.

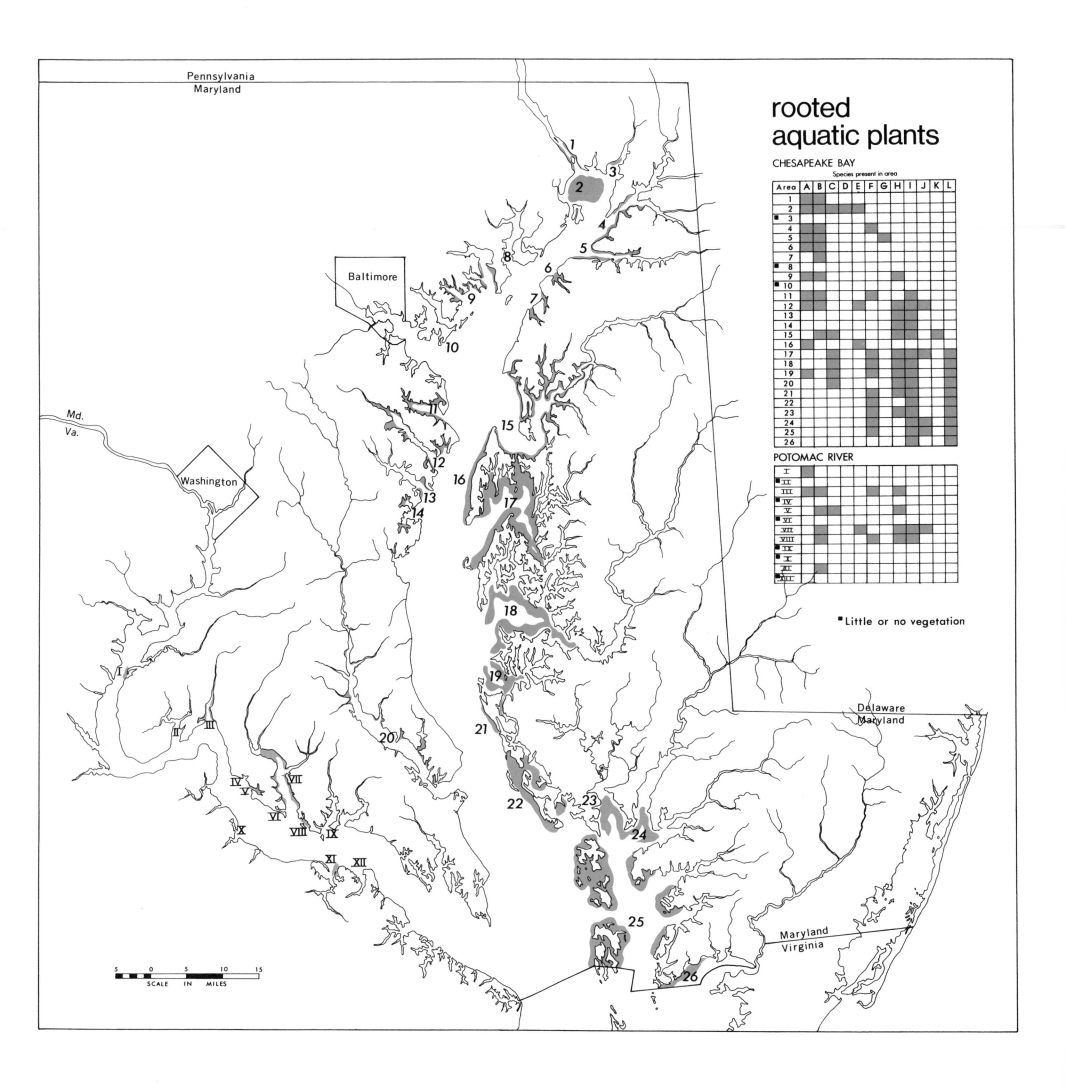

phytoplankton: microscopic plants

Phytoplankton (the word means green plant wanderers) are typically unicellular microscopic plants. They occur in both fresh and marine waters. Several important groups—such as diatoms, dinoflagellates, yellow-brown algae, green algae, and blue-green algae—occur in temperate estuaries. The diversity of species is very high, with the greatest number of species usually occurring in full-strength sea water. Many shapes and sizes are known. The cell wall of the diatom is composed of silica, which dissolves slowly; hence, large accumulations deposited on the bottom during geological times have formed what is called "diatomaceous earth." Other phytoplankton have different cell wall compositions and ornamentations. Many forms have small threadlike structures known as flagella, which aid in locomotion.

Phytoplankton are cosmopolitan and have special significance in the biological and geochemical cycles of the sea. Nutrition is varied. Some forms are autotrophic (photosynthetic), so that they are able to fix inorganic carbon dioxide into organic matter with the consequent liberation of oxygen. Others are heterotrophic (gain energy from dissolved organic compounds) or phagotrophic (feed on small particulate matter). The autotrophic forms, which possess the green pigment called chlorophyll, usually predominate and form the basis of the food web. Frequently, other pigments mask the chlorophylls, and the cells appear to be dark brown or yellow in color.

The distribution of phytoplankton in time and space is governed by the complex interaction of several important factors—light, temperature, nutrients, and herbivore (zooplankton) abundance. Cell division is rapid, and some phytoplankton can divide several times per day. Thus, a relatively scarce form can quickly gain dominance over associated forms when conditions change to favor it. Large blooms may discolor the water, and dense populations of some forms such as dinoflagellates can produce a dark red color in the water. Some dinoflagellates form a potent toxin, especially in tropical marine waters.

Distribution of the phytoplankton in Maryland's Chesapeake Bay is represented on the maps here not by individual phytoplankton species but by the total phytoplankton standing crop. This can be estimated from the concentration of a certain type of chlorophyll designated as chlorophyll *a* and measured as milligrams per cubic meter of water. Concentrations of chlorophyll *a* on the accompanying maps are measured from the euphotic zone, that portion of the water column near the surface where penetration of light is sufficient for plants to carry on photosynthesis effectively. Vertical differences in the concentration of chlorophyll *a* are not shown but are more important down-Bay. Deeper water, below the euphotic zone, contains phytoplankton cells, but they do not synthesize organic material autotrophically. However, some heterotrophic growth probably occurs.

Concentration of phytoplankton occurs in certain areas during the warm season, probably as the result of more favorable high temperature coupled with reduced flushing effects in low-salinity areas. Other factors may be involved. The large map illustrates this summer pattern.

The general pattern of summer concentrations of chlorophyll *a* which is plotted for the mainstream of the Bay and the Potomac and Patuxent Rivers probably will prove to be similar in other tributaries.

Data are available for many of the unmapped tributaries, but they are not readily transferable to this particular map. Beyond this, there is a great need for studies on the individual phytoplankton species and their contribution to the food web.

D. A. F.

Sources: Flemer (1970); Whaley *et al.* (1966).

Winter distribution of chlorophyll *a* in the euphotic zone. With less phytoplankton activity in winter months, there is a lower concentration of chlorophyll *a* (1–20 milligrams per cubic meter). This lighter phytoplankton crop is fairly uniformly distributed throughout the Chesapeake Bay from the mouth to the Susquehanna Flats.

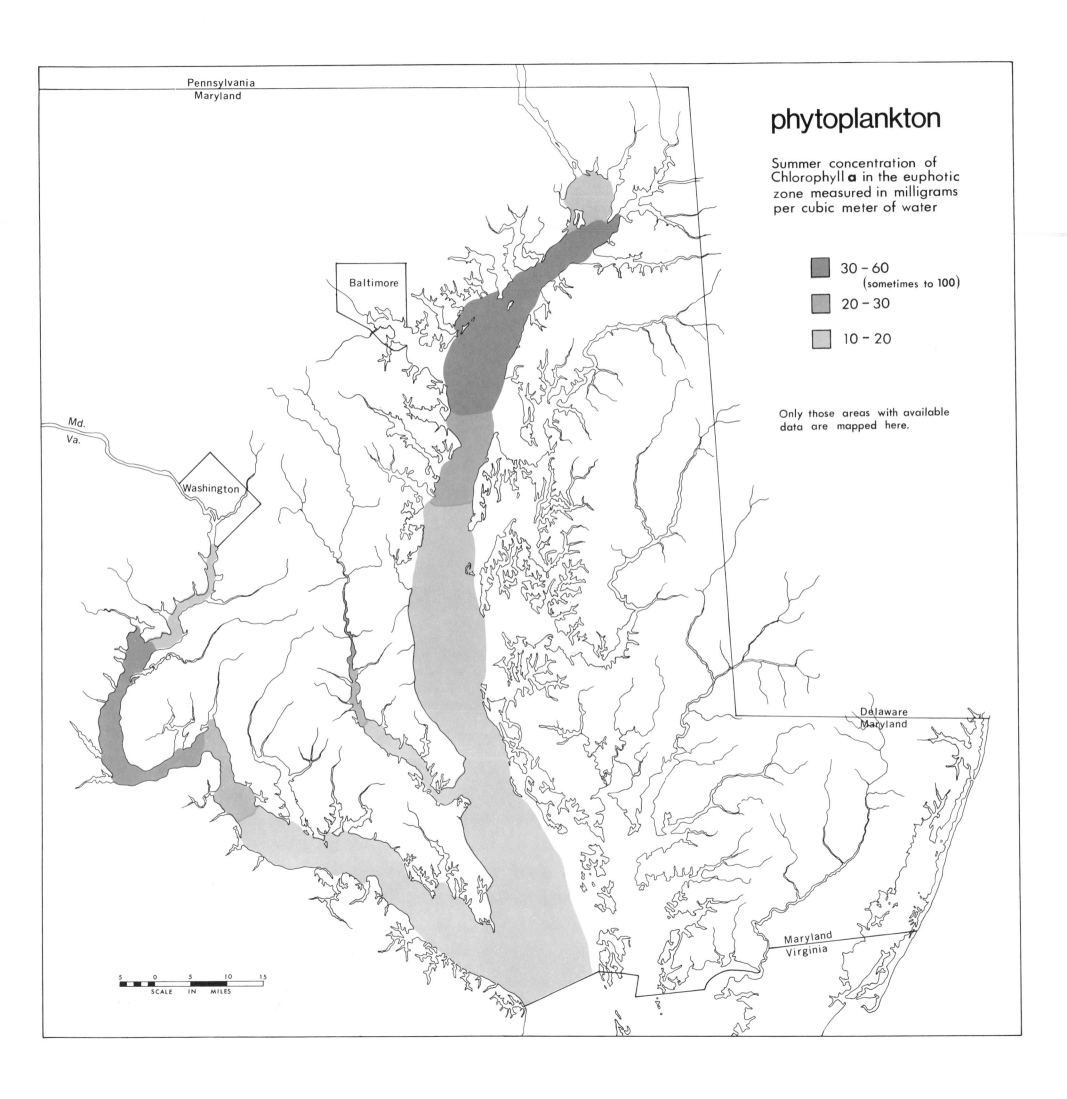

phytoplankton

Summer concentration of
Chlorophyll **a** in the euphotic
zone measured in milligrams
per cubic meter of water

- 30 – 60
  (sometimes to 100)
- 20 – 30
- 10 – 20

Only those areas with available
data are mapped here.

Pennsylvania
Maryland

Baltimore

Md.
Va.

Washington

Delaware
Maryland

Maryland
Virginia

5   0   5   10   15
SCALE   IN   MILES

copepods: microscopic animals

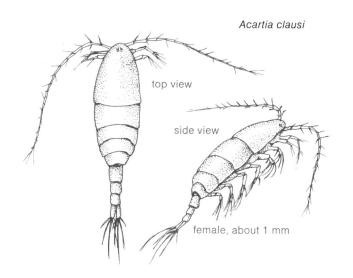

Acartia clausi

top view

side view

female, about 1 mm

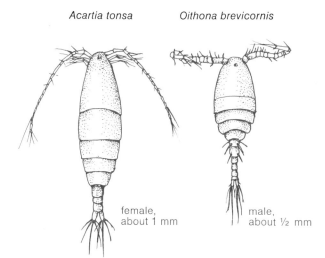

Acartia tonsa

Oithona brevicornis

female, about 1 mm

male, about ½ mm

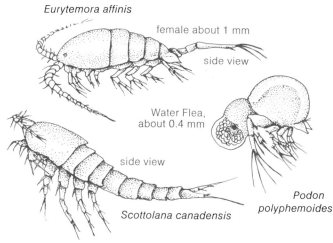

Eurytemora affinis

female about 1 mm

side view

Water Flea, about 0.4 mm

side view

Scottolana canadensis

Podon polyphemoides

These microscopic crustaceans, relatives of the crabs, are members of the order Copepoda and are considered by many to be the most abundant group of animals on earth. They are found throughout the world's oceans. A single cubic meter of water in the Chesapeake Bay may, at times, contain more than three million of these tiny creatures. There are three suborders of copepods, with three different body shapes and three slightly different methods of feeding. These are the Calanoida, the Cyclopoida, and the Harpacticoida. Most copepods are herbivores or omnivores, but some are strictly carnivores. There are about thirty species in the Chesapeake Bay, but five principal species make up approximately 95 percent of the average standing crop. These five most abundant species are, in decreasing order of importance (based on total quantities produced): *Acartia tonsa* (Calanoida), *Eurytemora affinis* (Calanoida), *Scottolana canadensis* (Harpacticoida), *Acartia clausi* (Calanoida), and *Oithona brevicornis* (Cyclopoida). These copepods obtain most of their energy from eating plant material—for example, algae, bacteria, or decomposing marsh grass—even though some of them are omnivores. The copepods are in turn eaten by virtually every larger organism in the Bay except shellfish. Even the shellfish may depend on them to some extent, since much of the organic matter deposited on the bottom of the Bay, and eaten by clams and oysters, is composed of waste material from the animals above.

Another microscopic crustacean, the water flea, *Podon polyphemoides,* is not a copepod but is related. It occurs in the Chesapeake Bay in such densities that it too is an important food source.

Acartia tonsa

Acartia tonsa, a fast-growing copepod, is food for many fishes and jellyfishes. The species is distributed throughout the brackish- and salt-water portions of the Bay during the summer months. Numbers are commonly in excess of 100,000 per cubic meter of water, and occasionally in excess of 1 million per cubic meter. During the winter, this species is rare in the lower, more saline portions of the Bay and is absent from the upper portions. The largest numbers in winter occur in areas where the salinity is about 10–20 o/oo.

Eurytemora affinis

Eurytemora affinis, another fast-growing copepod, is food for white perch and the young of striped bass, herrings and shad, and anchovies. This species is particularly important because its greatest numbers occur at the same place and time as the newly hatched larvae of many species of fish. It is restricted to the upper limits of brackish water during the summer months, occurring in greatest numbers during March and April at salinities of 5–12 o/oo. As many as 3 million individuals per cubic meter of water have been observed, but 100,000–500,000 per cubic meter are more common densities.

Scottolana canadensis

Scottolana canadensis is restricted to areas of less than 15 o/oo salinity between May and October, and its densities range from 50,000 to 1,500,000 per cubic meter of water. Adults overwinter at the upper limits of brackish water. The adults of this species live on or near the bottom, while very young animals are generally concentrated near the surface. Adults are food for spot, anchovies, and other bottom-feeders.

Acartia clausi

Acartia clausi largely replaces *A. tonsa* in the lower portions of the Bay during the winter and early spring months. Densities in excess of 100,000 per cubic meter of water have been observed.

Oithona brevicornis

Oithona brevicornis is a small, slow-growing copepod found commonly in higher-salinity waters. Its greatest density, about 100,000 per cubic meter, is achieved from July through November.

Podon polyphemoides

Podon polyphemoides, the water flea, occurs in higher-salinity areas of the Bay, but not often at the mouth of the Bay. Densities range from 0 to 100,000 per cubic meter of water from May through July, and from 0 to 23,000 per cubic meter from October through February.

D. R. H.

Sources: Goodwin (1968); Heinle (1969),
Bosch and Taylor (1970).

Winter and spring distribution of *Acartia tonsa* and *Eurytemora affinis*. *Acartia tonsa* populations decline from summer highs, while *Eurytemora affinis* populations increase and are more widespread, particularly in March and April.

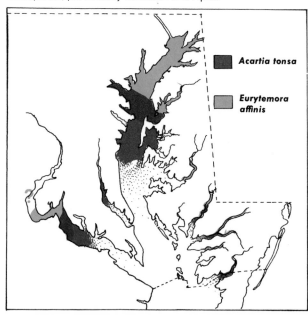

Acartia tonsa

Eurytemora affinis

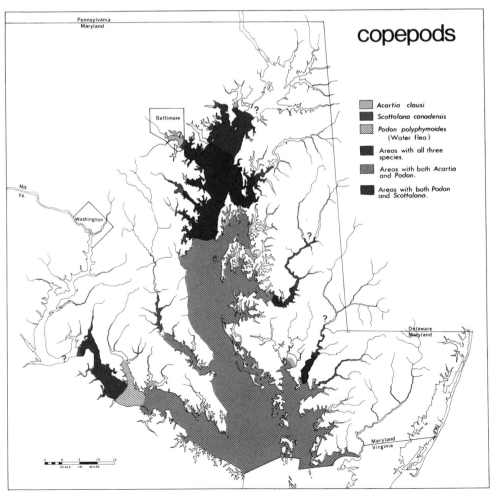

copepods

Summer–Fall
distribution of···

Acartia tonsa
May to September

Eurytemora affinis
June to November

Oithona brevicornis
July to November

Areas with both *A. tonsa*
and *Eurytemora.*

copepods

Acartia clausi

Scottolana canadensis

Podon polyphymoides
(Water flea)

Areas with all three
species.

Areas with both *Acartia*
and *Podon.*

Areas with both *Podon*
and *Scottolana.*

jellyfishes

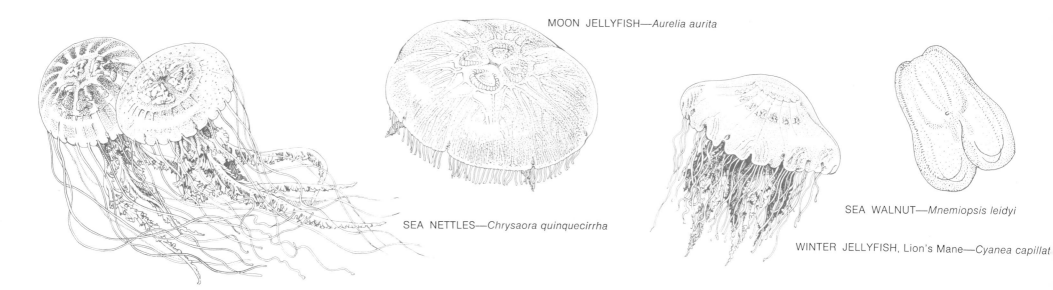

MOON JELLYFISH—*Aurelia aurita*

SEA NETTLES—*Chrysaora quinquecirrha*

SEA WALNUT—*Mnemiopsis leidyi*

WINTER JELLYFISH, Lion's Mane—*Cyanea capillat*

Several species of jellyfish, gelatinous animals that drift with the currents, occur in the Chesapeake Bay. Of these, the sea nettle is best known because of its great abundance and its ability to inflict painful stings with its long tentacles. Two other tentacled species, winter jellyfish and moon jellyfish, also are common. Winter jellyfish are not present during the swimming season, and so largely go unnoticed. Moon jellies, with their short tentacles, are less hazardous to swimmers.

All these medusae arise from the polyp forms of their species. Polyps are attached to the substrata (see drawing), while the medusae are free-floating.

Many smaller species of jellyfish without tentacles abound in the Bay. Ctenophores (called comb jellies or sea walnuts) are the largest of these (3–4 inches long). Sea walnuts feed voraciously on zooplankton, including crustacean and oyster larvae. Frequently their presence is more obvious at night, for they luminesce when disturbed.

Sea Nettle

The sea nettle is common in its large medusa form throughout the Bay and its tributaries, appearing as early as May, regularly present by late June, and lasting through November. Its peak abundance is reached during July and August. The number of sea nettles varies from year to year. In dense years, large aggregations of sea nettles are frequently seen in the water or in windrows along the shore. In light years, they are much less evident. Tidal estuarine areas are particularly infested. This jellyfish is much less common in Virginia waters, except in certain tributaries where populations approach those in the Maryland portion of the Bay. The sea nettle is well adapted to live in salinities of from 7 to 30 o/oo, but it will die in salinities lower than

5 o/oo. Sea nettles are usually milky white, but some have dark red bars on the bell.

The free-floating sea nettle medusae are released each spring from the sessile, or attached, polyp stage. The distribution of these polyps is limited by salinity to approximately a range of 7–25 o/oo. Polyps are found year-round except during the coldest months of extreme winters. Polyps are common in the tributaries of both Maryland and Virginia but are less common in the more salty areas of the Bay. White- to salmon-colored polyps, about one-eighth of an inch long, can frequently be found on the underside of empty oyster shells.

Winter Jellyfish

The orange or reddish winter jellyfish medusa occurs throughout the Bay from early winter to late spring. It is much more abundant in the southern part of the Bay than in Maryland waters. Winter jellyfish are sometimes found up tributaries to the extent of the tidal flow. The polyp stages are found from the Maryland-Virginia line southward.

Moon Jellyfish

This species of medusa, common from mid-summer to early fall, is distributed throughout the Bay and its tributaries. It too is much more common in the southern part of the Bay and is seen there earlier in the year. The smaller sizes of moon jellyfish are encountered more frequently in Virginia waters. Verified polyp stages have not been taken from the Bay, although the planulae (larvae) are able to set and form polyps at the mouth of the York River.

D. G. C.

Source: Schultz and Cargo (1971).

Sea Walnut

The sea walnut, *Mnemiopsis leidyi,* in the Chesapeake Bay penetrates to salinities of about 4 o/oo, but is confined to higher salinities during colder months. It is most abundant during late fall, winter, and early spring. Frequently the combined action of hydrological factors and swimming behavior result in large swarms. *Mnemiopsis* is found at a variety of depths, but tends toward greater depths during rough weather and in low salinities. Smaller individuals concentrate near the bottom and therefore may be carried upstream in an estuary.

Research on the distribution of ctenophores has been limited, so information is too sparse for mapping. The general areas of average 4 o/oo summer isohaline lines have been indicated on the map. Sea walnuts can be expected at least up to these limits.

J. W. B.

Source: Bishop (1972).

Polyp stage of the sea nettle forming cysts which will eventually give rise to other polyps.

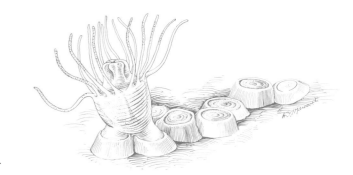

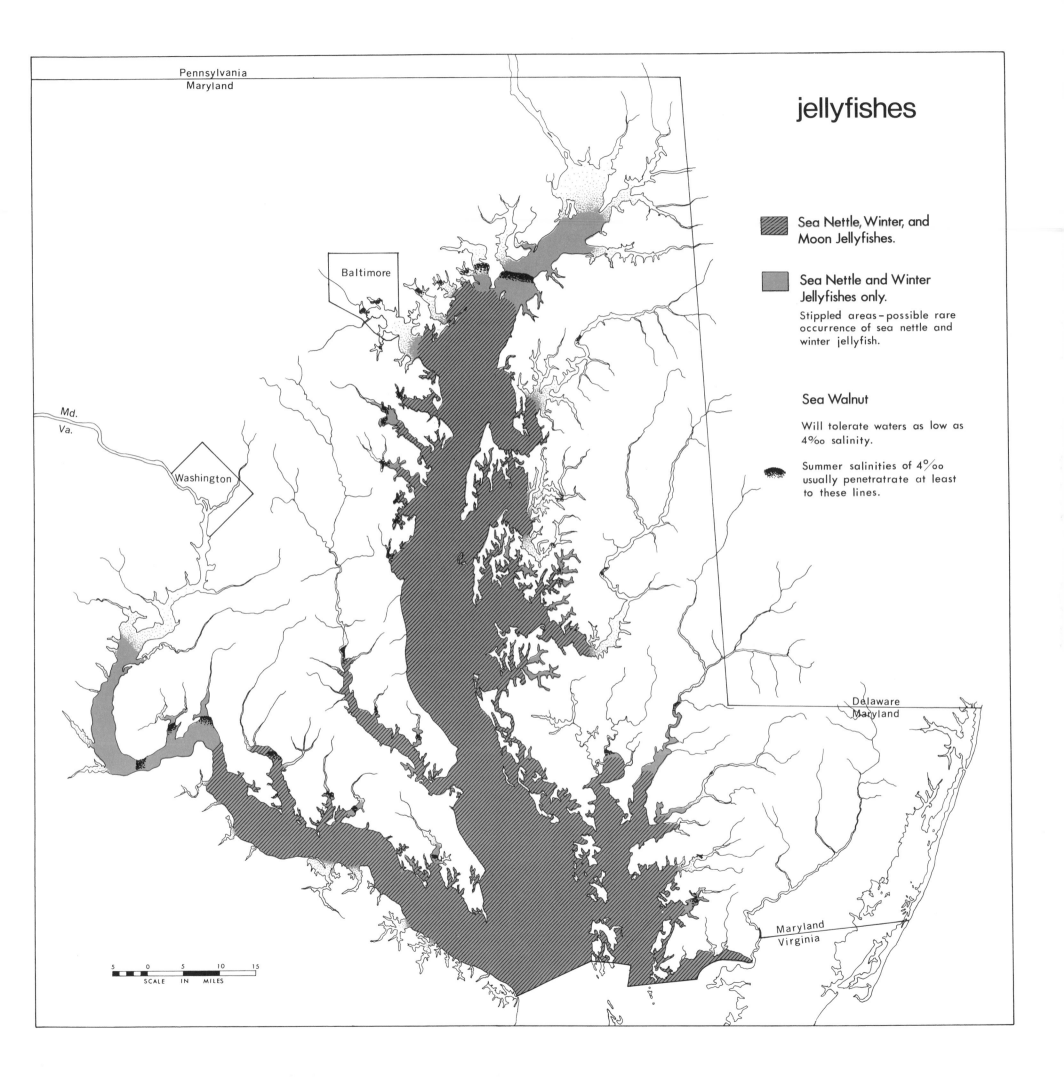

jellyfishes

Sea Nettle, Winter, and Moon Jellyfishes.

Sea Nettle and Winter Jellyfishes only.

Stippled areas - possible rare occurrence of sea nettle and winter jellyfish.

Sea Walnut

Will tolerate waters as low as 4‰ salinity.

Summer salinities of 4‰ usually penetratrate at least to these lines.

Pennsylvania
Maryland

Baltimore

Md.
Va.

Washington

Delaware
Maryland

Maryland
Virginia

5   0   5   10   15
SCALE   IN   MILES

clams

SOFT-SHELL CLAM, Manninose—*Mya arenaria*

HARD CLAM, Quahog, Little Neck, Cherrystone, Chowder Clam—*Mercenaria mercenaria*

BRACKISH-WATER CLAM—*Rangia cuneata*

There are many species of clams in Maryland's Chesapeake Bay. Most species are too small to be harvested, but all play their role in the ecology of the Bay. Of the three species mapped, two—the soft-shell clam and the hard clam—are harvested. The third, the brackish-water clam, is large enough (up to 2½ inches) to conceivably become a commercial species.

Soft-Shell Clam

The soft-shell clam industry has developed in Maryland only since 1951, when the invention of the hydraulic escalator dredge made it possible to harvest them economically in varying depths of water. Soft-shell clams are widely distributed throughout the Bay and its tributaries, but commercial concentrations occur only in certain areas between the Potomac and Chester Rivers.

Populations are densest in the tributaries and extend upriver to a salinity of about 5 o/oo. These clams are found only in sand or on sandy mud bottoms and generally in water less than 20 feet deep. Population densities continually change. Only the general area of soft-shell clam beds has been mapped; specific areas of high-density populations are not defined.

Hard Clam

Hard clams, another important commercial species, are limited to higher-salinity areas of the Chesapeake Bay. They are not found in water where the salinity is less than about 15 o/oo. In the Maryland portion of the Chesapeake Bay they are generally found in Tangier and Pocomoke Sounds. Hard clams are more abundant in Chincoteague and Sinepuxent Bays than in the Chesapeake.

The higher salinity of Chincoteague Bay has permitted the establishment of stable populations of hard clams, and there is a commercial and sports fishery for them there. Conditions are marginal for the species in the lower salinities of Tangier and Pocomoke Sounds. There is much fluctuation in the abundance and presence of hard clams in the upper parts of their range in these waters.

Near the Maryland-Virginia border, there have recently been enough *M. mercenaria* to support a small fishery based on the use of escalator harvesters.

Brackish-Water Clam

The brackish-water clam is a species first reported in Maryland waters in 1964. It is a southern species and is subjected to extensive winter die-off in the Chesapeake Bay. These clams are found in the Bay above the Bay Bridge, where salinities are low, and in the upper parts of certain tributaries in the central and lower regions of the Bay. They are generally found in low-saline water of from about 10 o/oo to about 1 or 2 o/oo. Their populations tend to be quite variable in this region.

As for the other clam species, the general area of their occurrence, rather than specifically delineated clam beds, has been mapped.

H. T. P., J. F. C., F. L. H., E. A. D.

Sources: Pfitzenmeyer and Drobeck (1964); Sieling (1956).

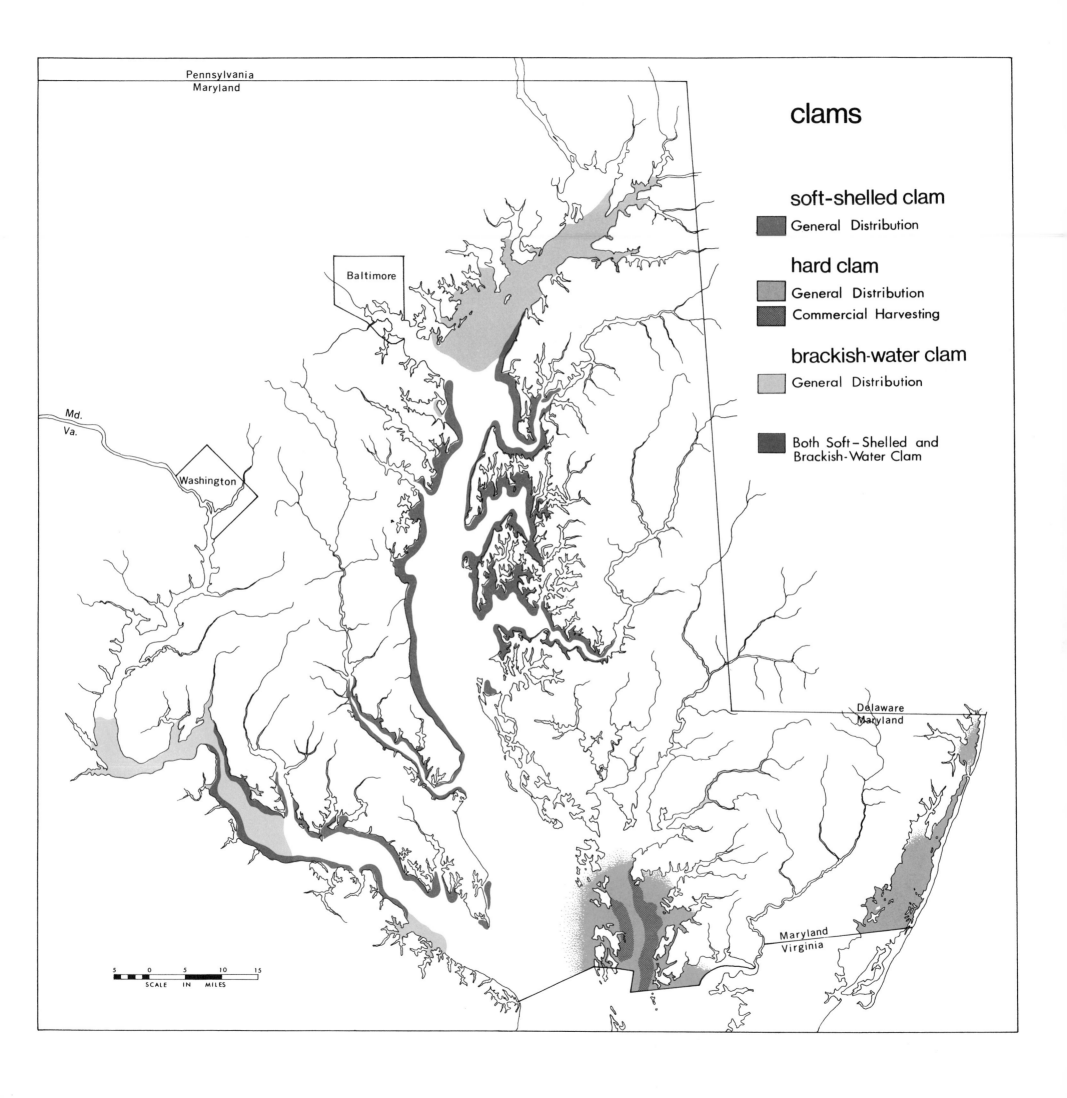

clams

soft-shelled clam
General Distribution

hard clam
General Distribution
Commercial Harvesting

brackish-water clam
General Distribution

Both Soft–Shelled and Brackish-Water Clam

Pennsylvania
Maryland

Baltimore

Md.
Va.

Washington

Delaware
Maryland

Maryland
Virginia

5   0   5   10   15
SCALE   IN   MILES

american oyster

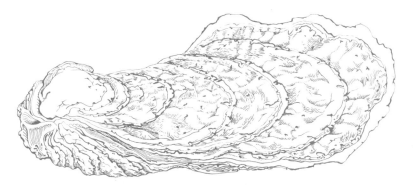

Crassostrea virginica

Full-grown Oyster   Oyster Shells with Spat

The commercial oyster of the east coast of North America has had a long history as an important species in the Chesapeake Bay. Although its numbers are now much reduced from those of precolonial times, the oyster is still distributed in the Bay from the Maryland-Virginia border to near the head of the Bay, as well as into most of the saltier tributaries upstream to a mean salinity of 7–8 o/oo. Although oysters can tolerate full ocean salinity, their distribution is increasingly limited by parasites, predators, and competitors that live in higher-salinity waters. In Chincoteague Bay, recent changes in ocean inlet size and location and resultant salinity increases have so favored some of these organisms that the number of oysters has been drastically reduced. Oysters require firm bottoms to prevent sinking and smothering, and they normally are found attached to shells, other live oysters, stones, or other hard objects. In the Chesapeake Bay, oysters are subtidal, and most occur in water between 8 and 25 feet deep. Seasonal deficiencies in dissolved oxygen prevent their establishment in most waters over 35 feet deep. *C. virginica* has been lost over much of its range because of overfishing and, to a lesser extent, siltation. Great accumulations of oyster shells are a significant bottom feature of the estuary. With their filter-feeding, live oysters, oyster "bars," rocks, or reefs support communities of organisms that are essential to the total ecology of the Chesapeake. The amount of successful oyster spawning, setting, and survival as small oysters, or "spat," varies greatly among the diverse habitats of the Chesapeake Bay. Some areas have such low reproductive potential that normal harvesting results in a depletion of stocks unless some artificial replenishment is employed. A few areas are self-sustaining if good harvesting practices are followed. Fortunately, some places produce a surplus of spat which can be transplanted as "seed" to areas having lower reproduction rates. Such transplanting is the basis for extensive rehabilitation efforts in which shells are placed on the bottom for the expected attachment of spat. Most, but not all, of both the actual and potential seed areas lie in parts of tributaries in which water movements result in the retention of larvae within the spawning area. However, many of these good seed areas are poor areas for growing oysters to market size. The young oysters, then, are taken up after a few months of growth and are moved to good growing areas. "Potential" seed-producing areas have adequate reproductive capacities but have not been used, for various special reasons, such as water depth, transport distance, and, in the case of Chincoteague Bay, the need for special protection from predators.

Extensive hydrographic and biological surveys by state and federal agencies have located oysters with greater accuracy than is feasible for most estuarine organisms. The distribution of oysters within the indicated areas on the map is far from uniform, and densities vary greatly. All habitats shown are areas that have had oysters in the recent past (about sixty years), although some sparsely populated bars are more potential than actual.

Extensive surveys by state and federal agencies, as well as continued monitoring by state management personnel, promise a more accurate location of seed areas than is possible on the scale of the present map.

E. A. D.

Sources: Frey (1946); Yates (1913);
U.S. Department of Commerce, Coast
and Geodetic Survey (1961); Spinner (1969).

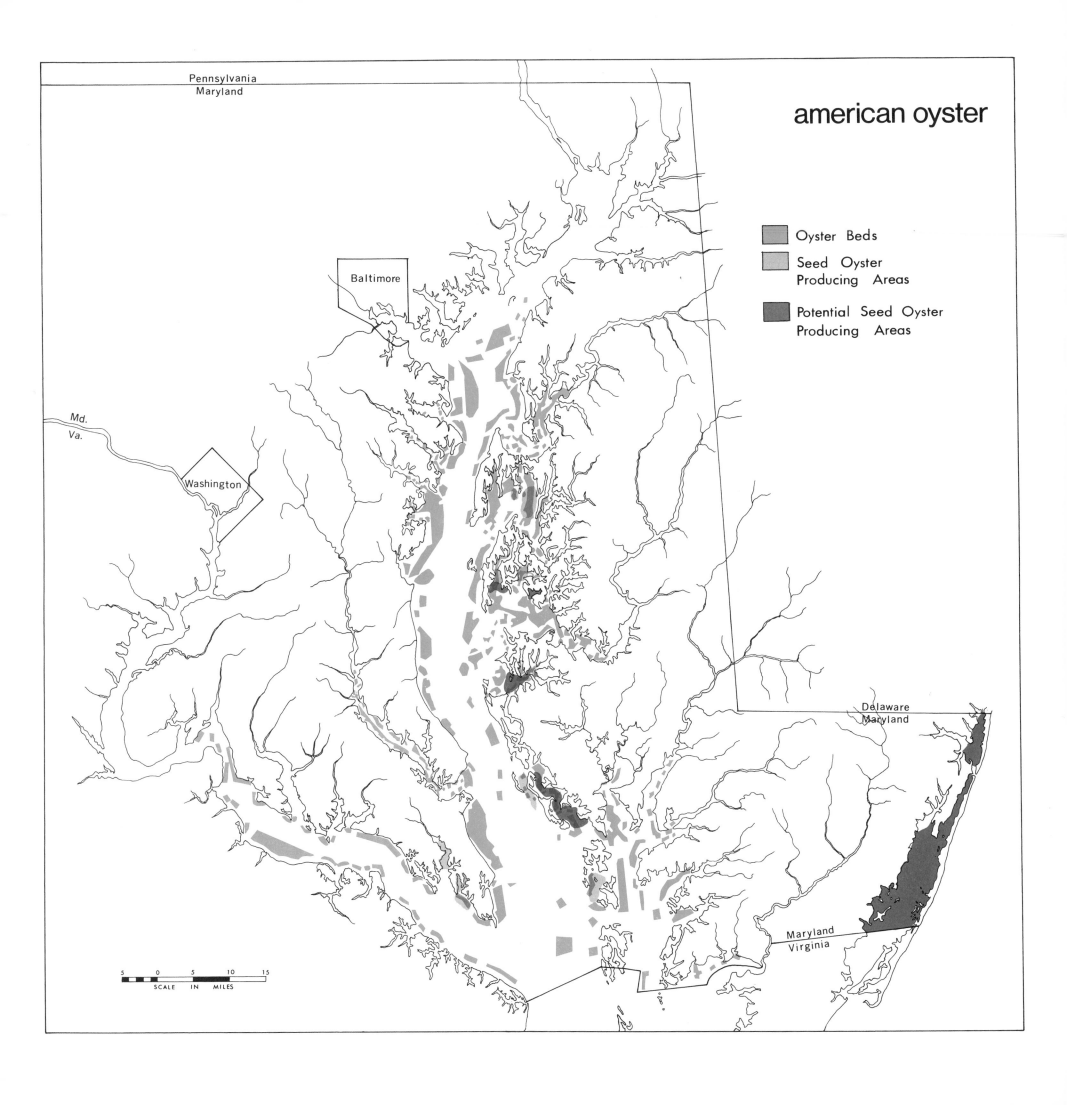

american oyster

Oyster Beds

Seed Oyster
Producing Areas

Potential Seed Oyster
Producing Areas

Pennsylvania
Maryland

Baltimore

Md.
Va.

Washington

Delaware
Maryland

Maryland
Virginia

5   0   5   10   15
SCALE   IN   MILES

oyster predators and parasites

OYSTER DRILLS, Screwborers

Urosalpinx cinerea

Eupleura caudata

Two predatory mollusks and two microparasites are prime enemies of the oyster in Maryland waters.

Predators

Urosalpinx cinerea and *Eupleura caudata,* closely related species of snails and both quite small (½–1 inch in diameter), are the principal predators of oyster beds. They bore small, round pinholes through the shells of oysters and consume the oyster through these holes.

In Maryland, oyster drills are serious predators only in the saltiest parts of the lower Tangier and Pocomoke Sounds and in Chincoteague Bay. The more abundant and larger *U. cinerea* extends up to a mean salinity of about 18 o/oo on the Eastern Shore, while the less tolerant *E. caudata* is not found where the mean salinity is below about 20 o/oo. Both species are found throughout Chincoteague Bay, but here, too, *E. caudata* is less abundant than *U. cinerea*. In the lower-salinity, marginal reaches of their habitats, snails are smaller than those in the more favorable environments downstream. Small drills can penetrate only small oysters; thus, they do less damage to mature oyster populations in the upstream areas. The distinctive egg cases of these snails, which are often seen on oyster shells and other substrates, can be useful indicators of their presence even when the adults are not taken in a sample. There is much fluctuation

in the populations of these drills in the marginal upstream portions of their range.

Parasites

MSX, *Minchinia nelsoni,* is a microscopic protozoan parasite of oysters present in the Chesapeake Bay and the lower reaches of its tributaries from near the mouth of the Choptank River southward and in Chincoteague Bay. MSX has seriously reduced oyster populations in the higher-salinity portions of its range (Pocomoke Sound and lower Tangier Sound) in Maryland. This pathogen was first identified in the Chesapeake area in the late 1950s and, although some local range extensions have been observed, it is not known whether or not it is completely new to the area. Although MSX can be devastating to oysters, infected oysters are not harmful to humans. A related species, *Minchinia costalis,* is found only on the seaside. High salinity (over 15 o/oo) favors the development of MSX. Oysters of all ages are vulnerable to infection, and host population density seems not to be as important in the epidemiology of this parasite as it is for Dermo (see below). Initial infections are seen in the epithelia of gills and other filtering organs; connective tissue is then invaded, and terminal infections show massive cell damage and breakdown of tissues.

Dermo, *Labyrinthomyxa marinum* (*Dermocys-*

tidium marinum), is a fungus parasite of oysters also found in the Bay and the lower reaches of its tributaries from near the mouth of the Choptank River southward. Like MSX, it is not harmful to humans. It is favored by high temperature, high salinity, and most especially by crowded host populations, which permit massive reinfections. Thus, peaks of infestation are reached in late summer and early fall. Infections spreading throughout the host population are accompanied by extensive breakdown of connective tissues. Young (under two years old) oysters seem not to be seriously affected by the parasite. In Maryland waters, Dermo causes significant, but not catastrophic, infections, with seasonal fluctuations depending upon climate and host population density. There is no evidence that this parasite has been recently introduced to this area; on the contrary, it is likely that it has been here for a long time. Other parasites morphologically similar to Dermo, but apparently very host-specific, have been seen in other bivalve mollusks in the Chesapeake Bay area. Dermo has been found in Chincoteague Bay, but it is not common there.

These parasites have been found throughout the area indicated on the map, although there is some fluctuation of occurrence, particularly in the upstream areas, where conditions are marginal for them.

Source (on predators): Carriker (1955). E. A. D.

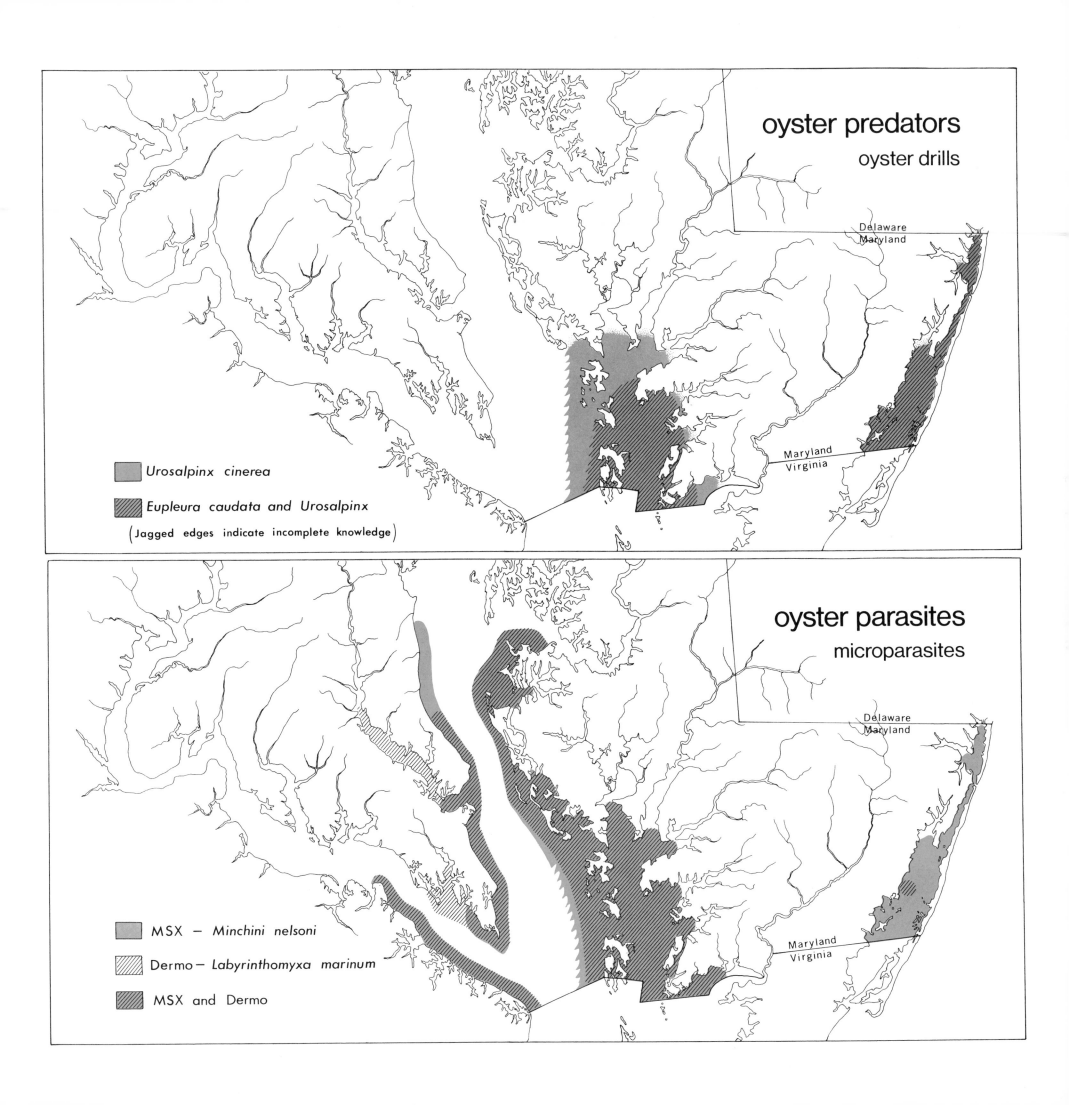

oyster predators

oyster drills

Delaware
Maryland

Maryland
Virginia

Urosalpinx cinerea

Eupleura caudata and Urosalpinx

(Jagged edges indicate incomplete knowledge)

oyster parasites

microparasites

Delaware
Maryland

Maryland
Virginia

MSX – Minchini nelsoni

Dermo – Labyrinthomyxa marinum

MSX and Dermo

blue crab

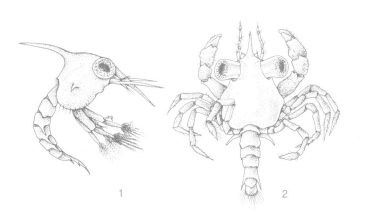

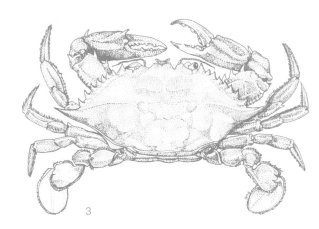

Callinectes sapidus

1. Zoeae
2. Megalopa, about 1/16 in
3. Adult

The blue crab is widely distributed along the Atlantic and Gulf coasts, but is most abundant and perhaps best known from the Chesapeake Bay.

It is truly an estuarine species, occurring from areas of nearly fresh water to full-strength ocean salinity.

The male blue crab generally will range much farther into low-salinity waters than the female. In Maryland, in the lowest-salinity areas of the upper Bay and its upper tributaries, males predominate, traveling even into the smallest creeks.

Females, on the other hand, tend to congregate farther downstream and down-Bay, where salinities are greater. Mating occurs from June through October in the middle and upper Bay and its tributaries. The peak of mating intensity is usually during July and August. After impregnation, the females migrate toward the lower Bay to the higher-salinity spawning grounds, not to return until the following spring, while the majority of males remain in the fresher waters, most overwintering in the muddy bottoms of deeper channel waters.

Blue crabs spawn in the high-salinity waters near the mouth of the Chesapeake during the summer and early fall months. The one to two million eggs laid by the female adhere to her undersurface and form the so-called sponge. The eggs hatch within a few weeks, releasing small semitransparent larvae, termed zoeae, which swim away and assume a planktonic existence.

Zoeae undergo several molts within approximately six weeks. The larva becomes more complex in body structure after each successive molt. The final zoeal molt produces a secondary larval form called a megalopa. The megalopa is about one-sixteenth to one-eighth of an inch long and looks somewhat like a tiny lobster, complete with claws. In contrast to the zoeae, the megalopae, although able to swim, tend to crawl along the bottom. The megalopae move up the estuary into lower-salinity waters, where they molt and become tiny, but recognizable, blue crabs. Crabs molt frequently during their first year, although growth is interrupted in the winter, when they undergo a semihibernation. By the age of twelve to sixteen months, crabs hatched in early summer have reached sexual maturity and legal size (5 inches). Crabs hatched from eggs spawned in late summer and early fall usually require from eighteen to twenty months to attain full legal size. The blue crab's life span is short, probably not more than three years.

The distribution of the adult blue crab as mapped reflects data from many years of observation, including a three-year intensive study at Chesapeake Biological Laboratory from 1968 through 1970. The general pattern is usually followed, but crabs are notorious for exceptions to the pattern and for sudden changes in availability to crabbers. Current research is focused on growth studies, on periodic fluctuations in stocks, and on developing techniques to induce crabs to shed in order to increase the availability of soft crabs.

R. L. L.

Sources: Churchill (1919); Lippson (1971); Van Engel (1958); Truitt (1939).

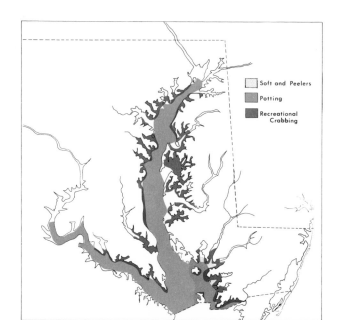

Soft and Peelers

Potting

Recreational Crabbing

HARVESTING THE BLUE CRAB

Blue crabs are an important commercial and sport resource in Maryland. Crabs are taken commercially by pots, trot lines, scrapes, dip nets, and, in limited areas, by crab traps. Crabs may be taken by these means from April 1 to December 31. Potting is legal only in the Bay proper and in the Potomac River, excluding their tributaries (see map).

Hard crabs constitute the major portion of the total poundage of crabs landed in Maryland. However, a small but intensive fishery specializes in harvesting the much-sought-after soft crab. Legal soft crabs are crabs which have just shed and measure a minimum of 3½ inches across the back, from the tip of one lateral spine to the other. Hard crabs must measure a minimum of 5 inches.

Sport or recreational crabbing is a favorite pastime with Marylanders and visitors to Chesapeake Bay. No figures are available on the actual number of crabs landed by sportsmen, but it is substantial.

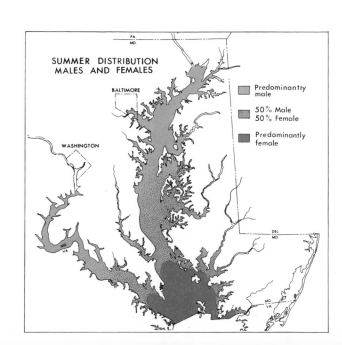

SUMMER DISTRIBUTION
MALES AND FEMALES

Predominantly male

50% Male
50% Female

Predominantly female

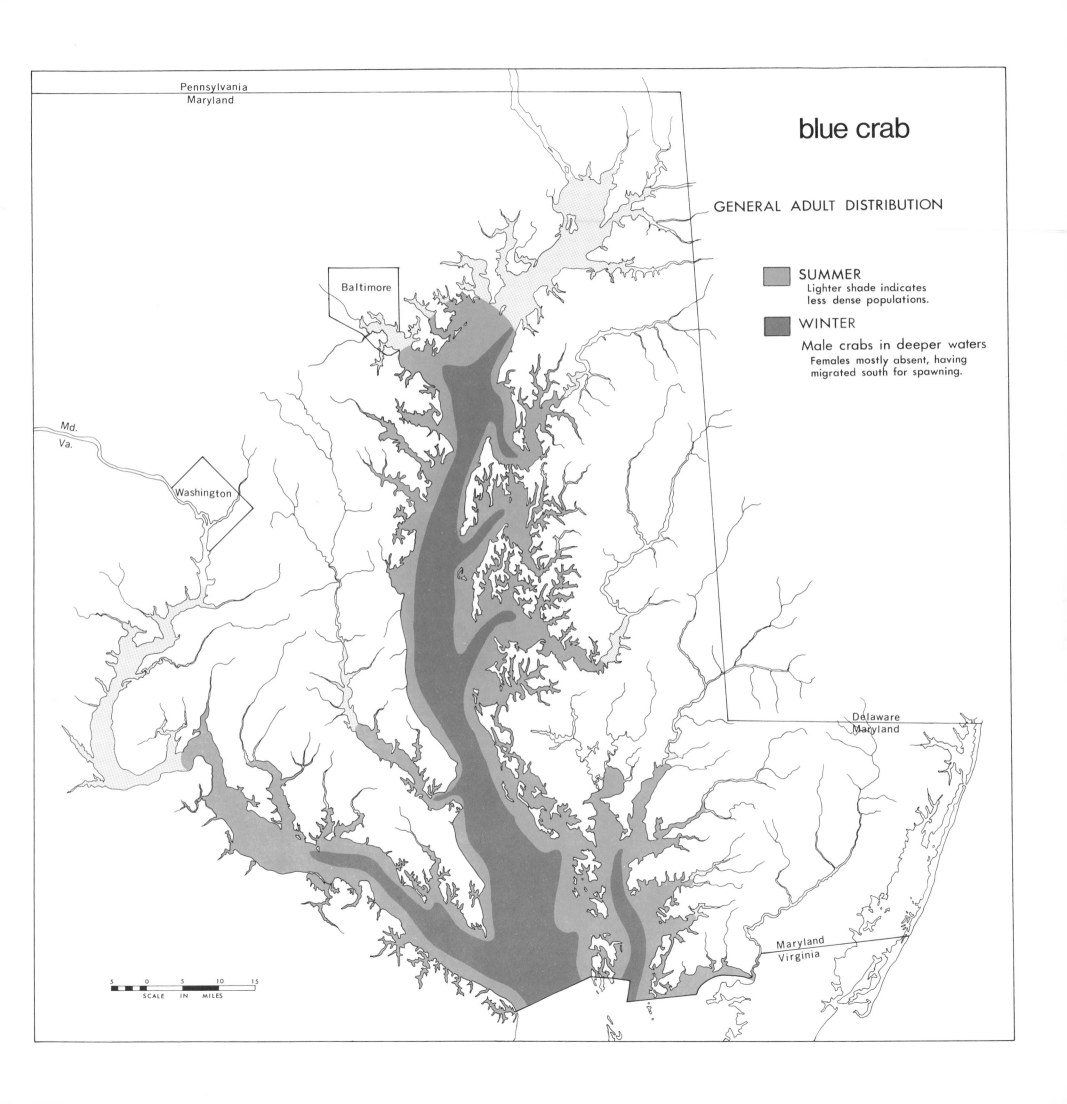

blue crab

GENERAL ADULT DISTRIBUTION

SUMMER
Lighter shade indicates
less dense populations.

WINTER

Male crabs in deeper waters
Females mostly absent, having
migrated south for spawning.

Pennsylvania
Maryland

Baltimore

Md.
Va.

Washington

Delaware
Maryland

Maryland
Virginia

5 0 5 10 15
SCALE IN MILES

herrings

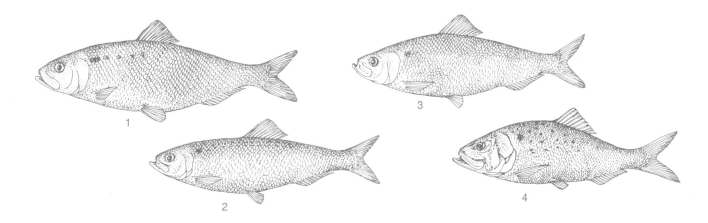

1. AMERICAN SHAD, Shad, White Shad—*Alosa sapidissima*
2. BLUEBACK HERRING, Glut Herring—*Alosa aestivalis*
3. ALEWIFE, Branch Herring—*Alosa pseudoharengus*
4. MENHADEN, Bunker—*Brevoortia tyrannus*

Blueback, alewife, and shad, the most abundant herrings in the Chesapeake Bay, are found throughout all parts of the Bay and its tributaries, with their distribution being dependent on the season of the year. Herrings are anadromous fish, which means that they leave the ocean and swim upstream to fresh water to spawn in the late winter and early spring months.

Shad

Shad are the first to enter the estuaries, usually appearing in upper river areas as early as February. Spawning continues through April, usually occurring in tidal fresh water. After spawning, adult shad return to the sea, leaving the Bay by June. Young shad, however, remain in the Bay and its tributaries throughout the summer, some returning to the sea in the fall, others remaining in the Bay for their first winter. Immature shad remain at sea for from three

to six years, until maturity, when they return again to the estuaries to spawn. Tagging and the study of markings on shad scales have shown that the mature fish can return with marvelous accuracy to the site at which it was spawned.

Alewives and Blueback Herring

Alewives and blueback herring enter the spawning grounds a little later than the shad. Alewife runs usually occur from March through April, blueback runs from the last half of April through the first half of May. After spawning, adults descend the rivers to the lower estuaries and Bay, where they spend the summer months. As cold weather approaches, they either move to deep Bay waters or return to sea. The young from the year's hatch follow this same general pattern, except for remaining in the upper estuaries for a longer period of time in spring and summer.

Atlantic Menhaden

Menhaden, a herring-like fish closely related to the other three species, is also an abundant Bay fish. Unlike anadromous herrings, they spawn in the ocean, so no large "spawning" runs occur in the spring months. However, rapidly growing menhaden larvae soon migrate from the ocean to the upper estuaries into fresh and brackish water, where they are found in great numbers during the spring months. These juveniles commonly emigrate to the sea after spending their first summer in the estuaries. Menhaden are found in the Chesapeake Bay throughout the year; larger numbers congregate in shoal areas during the summer, and smaller numbers overwinter in deeper waters, most having returned to the sea.

M. L. W., A. J. L.

Sources: Hildebrand and Schroeder (1929); Leim and Scott (1966); Mansueti and Hardy (1967).

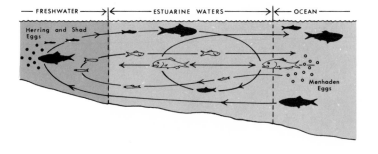

Diagram of the pattern of movement of various stages in the life of herrings (shad, alewife, blueback) and menhaden. Herring eggs are spawned in fresh or tidal-fresh waters; menhaden eggs are spawned in ocean salinities. Larvae and juveniles of all species utilize the upper tributaries, from fresh water to brackish water. The young and adults of all species utilize mid-estuarine areas in summer (although adult shad leave the Bay by early summer). Some remain in deeper waters through the winter; others return to sea.

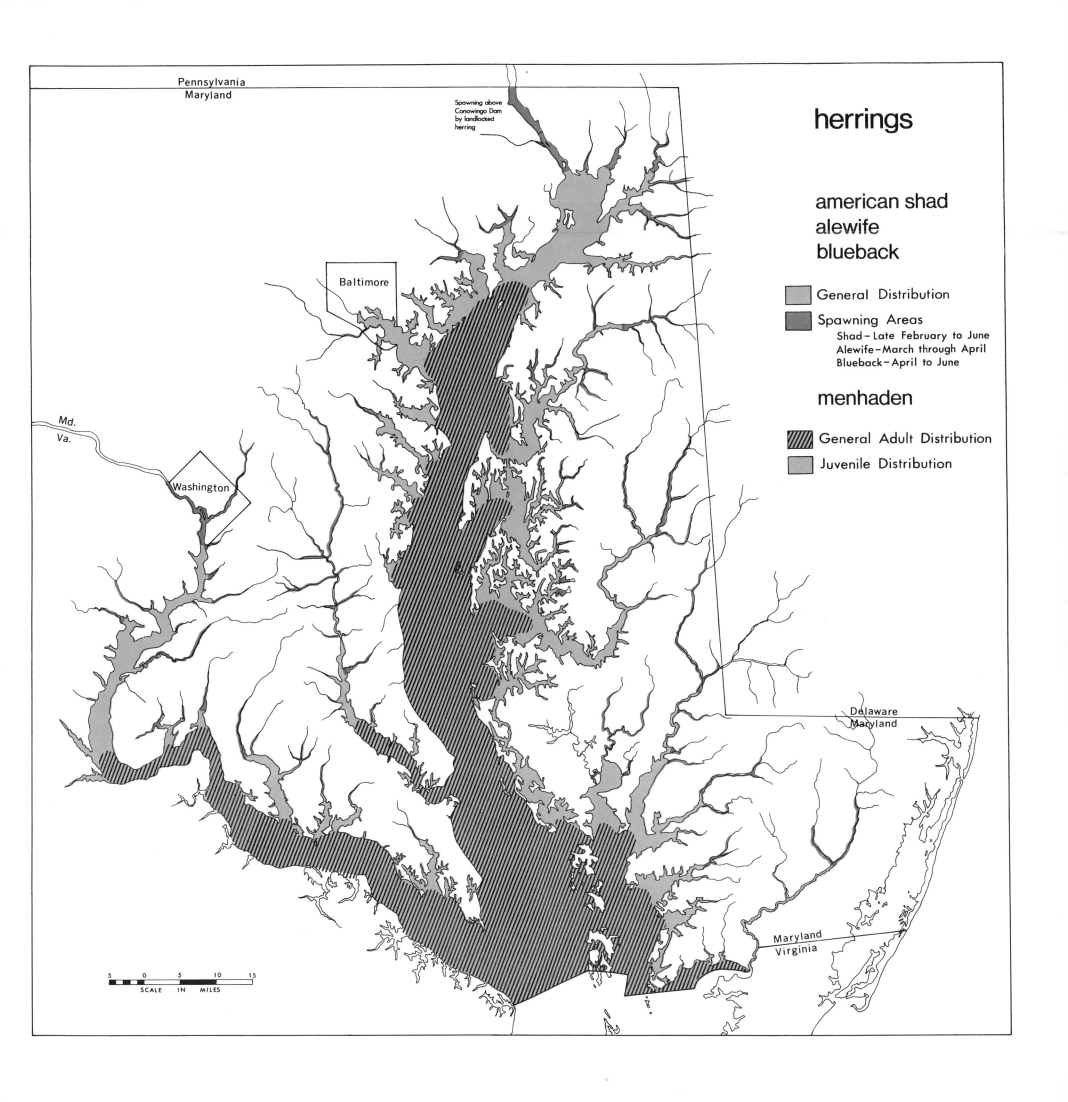

herrings

american shad
alewife
blueback

General Distribution

Spawning Areas
Shad – Late February to June
Alewife – March through April
Blueback – April to June

menhaden

General Adult Distribution

Juvenile Distribution

Pennsylvania
Maryland

Spawning above
Conowingo Dam
by landlocked
herring

Baltimore

Md.
Va.

Washington

Delaware
Maryland

Maryland
Virginia

5   0   5   10   15
SCALE   IN   MILES

american eel

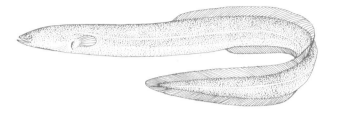

Anguilla rostrata

The American eel is an elongate, bony fish with slimy skin. Minute scales, usually overlooked, do not appear until the third year, when the fish is 6–8 inches long. Eels do not have typical ventral fins but rather a single, soft-rayed fin, which is continuous along the back, around the tail, and forward on the belly.

American eels are widely distributed throughout the Chesapeake Bay and its tributaries. In Maryland, they are found in practically all rivers up into fresh water and are often very abundant. A small but intensive fishery exists for eels in the Chesapeake Bay, primarily for use as crab bait. Watermen set out characteristic cylindrical eel pots in the spring; the eels are salted and later used principally to bait crab trotlines. Eels are not generally sought for food in this area; however, closely related species are highly favored in Europe and Asia.

Eels are voracious, omnivorous feeders and are known to prey on or scavenge crabs, shrimp, fish, mollusks, worms, and grasses.

A number of ichthyologists have studied the life history of the American eel and its distribution, and, consequently, a large volume of information has been assembled; but there is still much that is unknown or imperfectly known, such as the exact spawning area and the nature of the eggs. The eggs, which are probably pelagic, hatch into elongate larvae with large teeth. The larvae soon develop into the leptocephalus stage, which was at one time considered to be a different species of fish. Leptocephalus larvae are flat, ribbon-shaped, and tapered at both ends and are similar in shape to a leaf. The larval eels either are carried by water currents or swim toward the Atlantic coast of North America. During the approximately one year required for their migration, they transform into the elver stage. The elvers, or "grass eels," are the transitional form between the leptocephalus larvae and the completely metamorphosed eels. The elver's body narrows and becomes more eel-like, and the skin is at first unpigmented and transparent. It is at this stage that the elvers appear at the mouths of estuaries and begin to ascend the bays and tributaries, where they finally transform into pigmented eels. The young eels remain in the estuaries for several years. Mature females may attain a length of 4 feet and average 2½–3 feet, while the males are smaller and probably do not exceed 2 feet. In the fall, as eels approach maturity, they leave the rivers and estuaries and begin their long migration to the southwestern Atlantic, in the region of the Sargasso Sea, where it is thought that spawning occurs.

R. L. L.

Sources: Bertin (1956); Bigelow and Schroeder (1953); Eales (1967); Hildebrand and Schroeder (1927); Leim and Scott (1966).

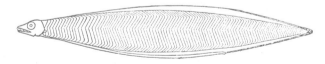

A leptocephalus larvae of the American eel, about 2 inches long. Drawing from Bigelow and Shroeder (1953).

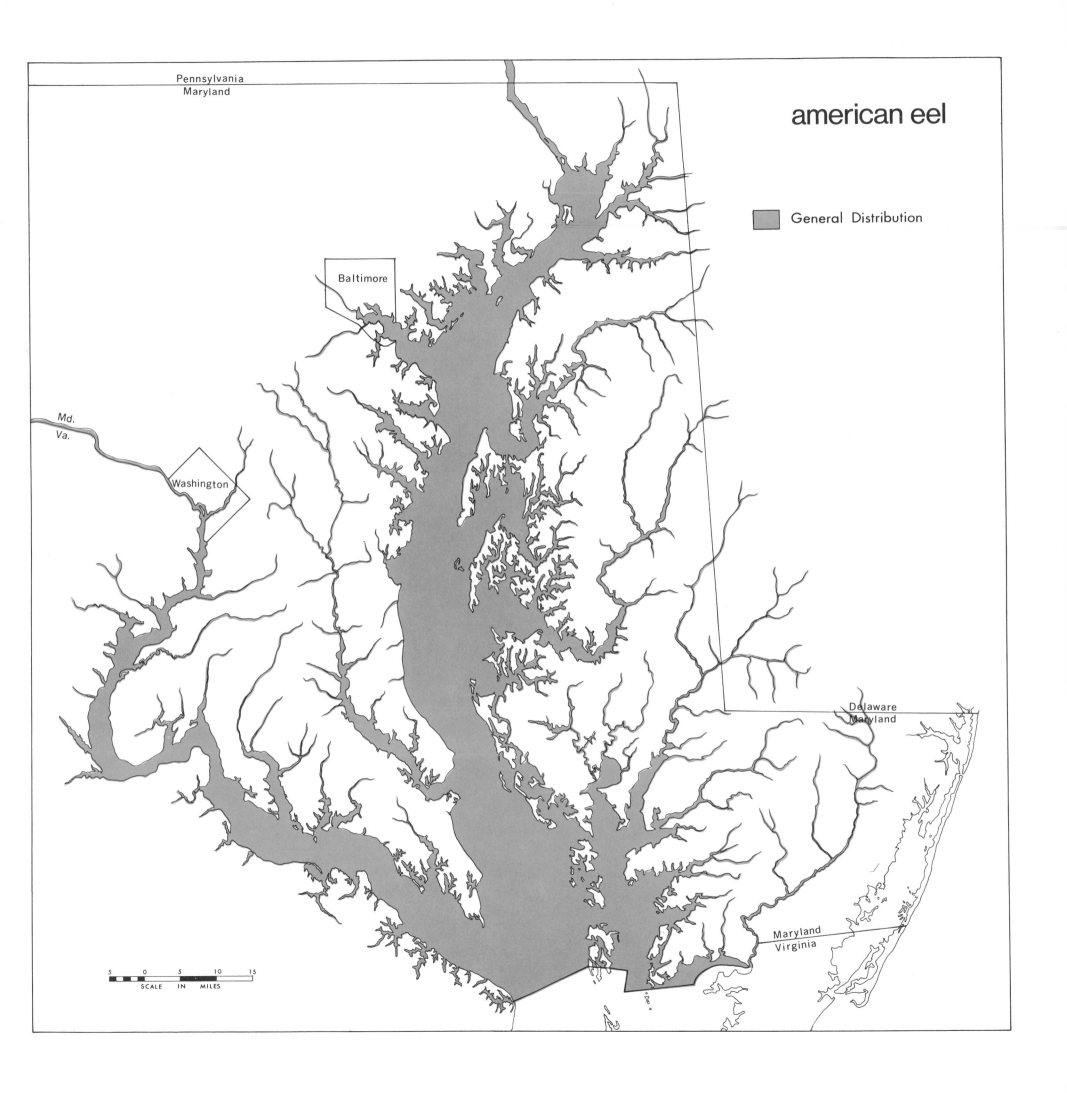

american eel

General Distribution

Pennsylvania
Maryland

Baltimore

Md.
Va.

Washington

Delaware
Maryland

Maryland
Virginia

5   0   5   10   15
SCALE   IN   MILES

catfishes

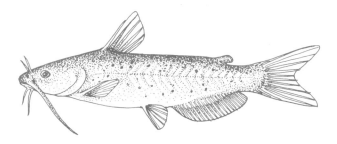

Channel Catfish—*Ictalurus punctatus*

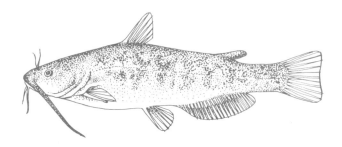

Brown Bullhead—*Ictalurus nebulosus*

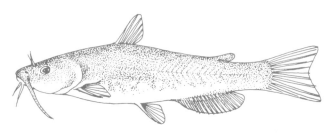

White Catfish—*Ictalurus catus*

Catfishes, easily recognized by their characteristic "whiskers" or barbels, are found in almost all fresh and brackish waters of Maryland. Although essentially fresh-water fishes, they readily adapt to salinities of up to 5–6 o/oo, and will tolerate salinities to about 10 o/oo. Catfish are bottom-feeders, and show a preference for deeper holes and still pools. They often form schools.

Of the three common species in Maryland's Chesapeake Bay system, brown bullheads and white catfish are the most widespread, being found in almost every tributary and stream. Channel catfish, on the other hand, are restricted to two areas, the upper Bay and Susquehanna River area and the upper Potomac River. They have been stocked in many other tributaries, but populations have not become established. Channel catfish prefer deeper channel waters and usually do not penetrate as far upstream as brown bullheads, which are commonly found in these more shallow, muddy waters.

Channel catfish are the predominant species in both the upper Bay and Susquehanna, although many white catfish are found in the Northeast River. In the Potomac below Washington all three species show a similar distribution, but brown bullheads are most abundant. Above Great Falls, however, channel catfish predominate, brown bullheads are scarce, and white catfish are absent.

Brown bullheads and white catfish spawn in late spring (May–June); the spawning season of channel catfish is a little earlier and more protracted. The large, heavy eggs are laid in adhesive clumps, usually in nests built by the parents. The eggs and larvae are guarded by a parent, usually the male. After leaving the nest, juvenile catfish congregate in dense schools for a period of time.

The general distribution of catfishes is well known, but the seasonal distribution and patterns of movement of life-history stages are not as well documented.

J. G. B., A. J. L.

Source: Mansueti and Hardy (1967).

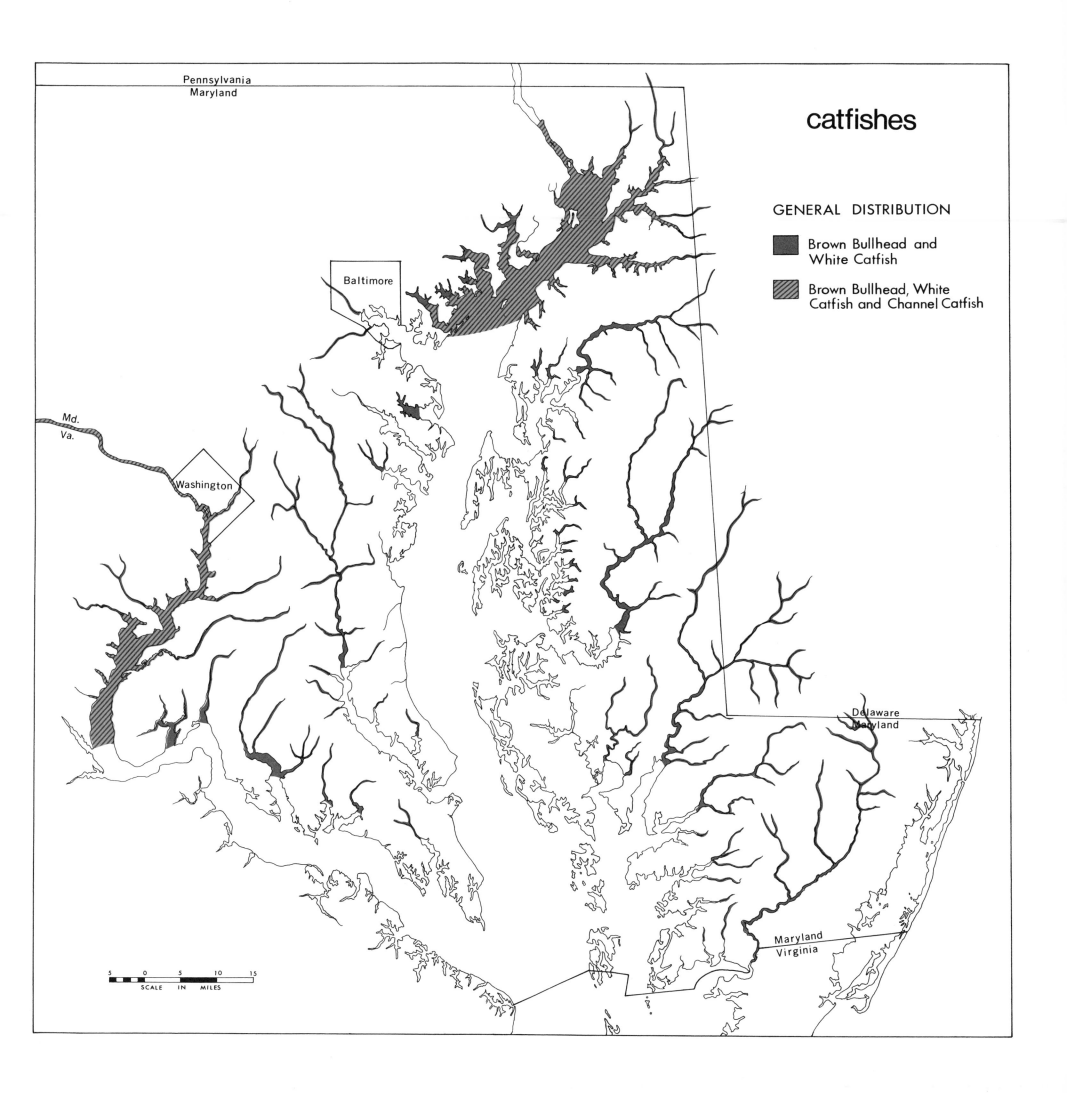

catfishes

GENERAL DISTRIBUTION

Brown Bullhead and
White Catfish

Brown Bullhead, White
Catfish and Channel Catfish

Pennsylvania
Maryland

Baltimore

Md.
Va.

Washington

Delaware
Maryland

Maryland
Virginia

5 0 5 10 15
SCALE IN MILES

white perch

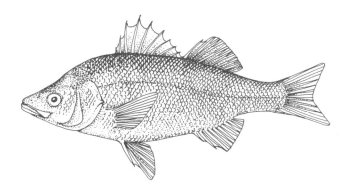

Morone americana

White perch are resident, semi-anadromous fish in the Chesapeake Bay. An ubiquitous, abundant species favored by both sport and commercial fishermen, they can be found in all brackish and tidal fresh-water areas at one time or another. Although distributed throughout the Bay system, discrete white perch populations apparently remain within specific tributaries. There appear to be indigenous populations in many rivers—the Potomac, Patuxent, Choptank, and Nanticoke, for example. However, within each particular estuary (river or the Chesapeake Bay proper), definite seasonal migratory patterns occur.

As early as March, ripe individuals move upstream to tidal fresh water or nearly fresh water to spawn, remaining there often until early June. The map shows generalized spawning regions. Favored within these regions are areas where the slightly heavier-than-water, adhesive white perch eggs will find suitable substrate for attachment, such as shallow streams with overhanging tree branches and fallen limbs, or deeper-water areas with firm, sandy bottoms.

After spawning, adults move randomly within their estuary system, with the larger fish more frequently tending to localize downstream.

After hatching, the larvae are concentrated in rich nursery areas close to the fresh-water/salt-water interface. As they grow, young white perch gradually move downstream and into shallow beach zones to feed for their first summer and fall. As winter approaches, the water cools, and white perch, both adults and juveniles, swim into regions deeper than 30–40 feet, where the water is slightly warmer, to move with and feed upon other bottom fauna.

Information on the distribution of white perch is well substantiated, for much research has been done on this species. It must be noted, however, that on the maps the spawning areas of the Potomac River tributaries in Virginia are not shown. Also, the area of major winter concentrations does not imply an absolute boundary.

D. E. R., H. I. K., A. J. L.

Sources: Mansueti (1961, 1964); Hildebrand and Schroeder (1927).

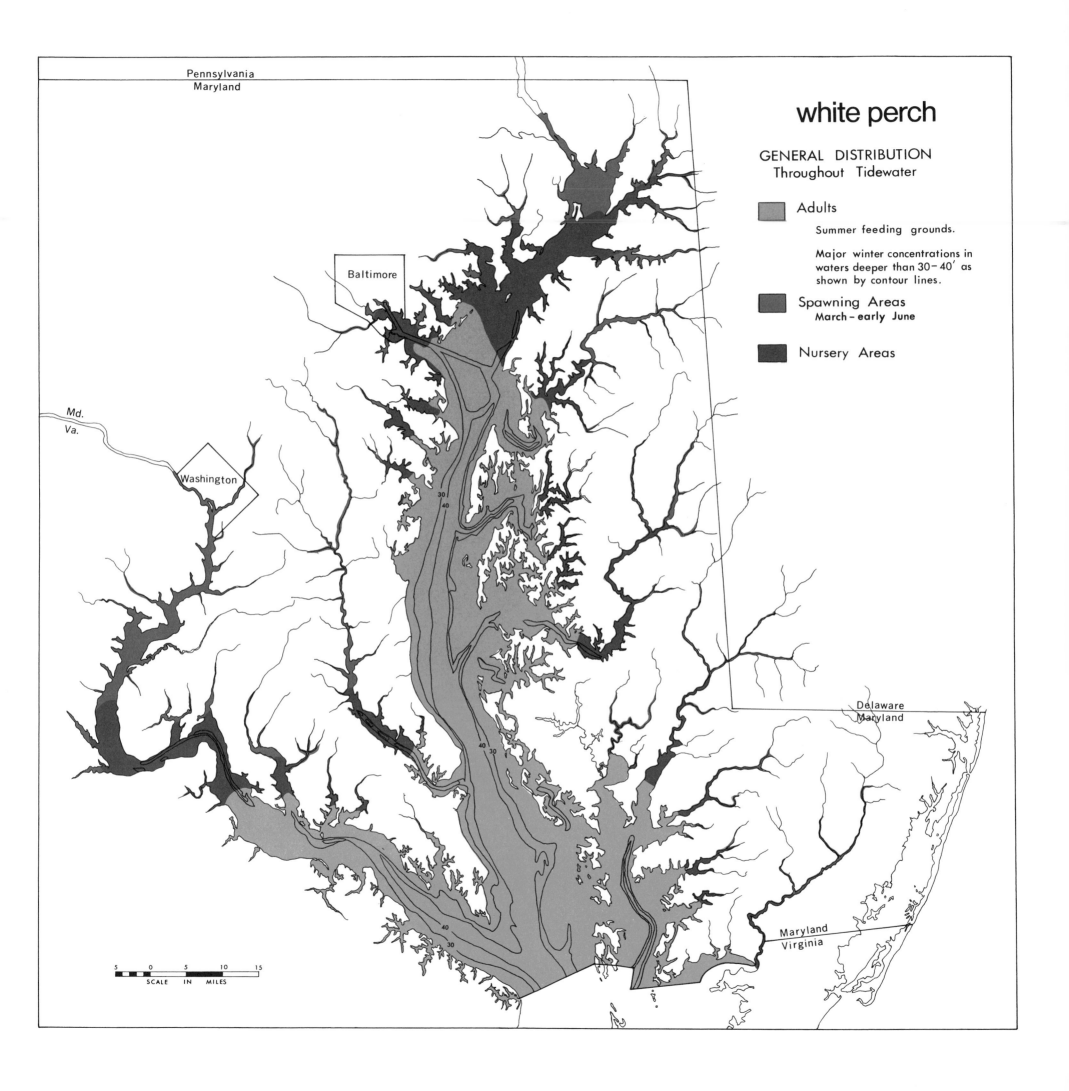

white perch

GENERAL DISTRIBUTION
Throughout Tidewater

Adults

Summer feeding grounds.

Major winter concentrations in
waters deeper than 30–40' as
shown by contour lines.

Spawning Areas
March – early June

Nursery Areas

Pennsylvania
Maryland

Baltimore

Md.
Va.

Washington

Delaware
Maryland

Maryland
Virginia

30
40

40
30

40
30

5   0   5   10   15
SCALE   IN   MILES

striped bass rock rockfish

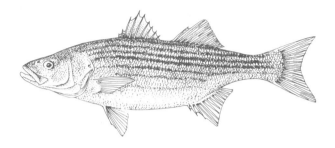

Morone saxatilis

The striped bass, or rockfish, is the most valuable and important fish in Maryland's Chesapeake Bay. Prized by both sport and commercial fishermen, it is a highly tolerant species found throughout the Bay proper and most of its major tributaries, even into tidal fresh water.

Adult striped bass show definite patterns of movement during three different seasons. During winter, they tend to migrate down-Bay and down the rivers to the deeper waters, where they over-winter in depths greater than 30 feet. They are highly susceptible to temperature changes, and, if a warming trend occurs, they will move out of these deeper waters. Although their activity decreases during the colder months, striped bass will continue to feed and travel to some extent.

As the spawning season arrives, April–June, ripe fish move up the Bay and its tributaries to the spawning areas, which are located in tidal-fresh or slightly brackish waters. Only tributaries with a strong river flow are suitable. Striped bass eggs require a certain amount of turbulence to keep afloat. Striped bass apparently have a strong homing instinct, for they return to the same rivers to spawn in successive years.

In Maryland, there are eleven general spawning areas. Spawning occurs in the region of the fresh-water/salt-water interface. The location of the interface fluctuates according to the amount of rainfall. Adult striped bass remain upstream throughout most of the spawning season, then gradually move downstream to the lower reaches of the tributaries and throughout the Bay proper.

The summer season, July–October, is spent actively feeding, with schools concentrating more along the shoal areas. Many striped bass remain within their own tributaries; others move out into the Bay and often travel great distances.

In late winter and spring, some larger striped bass migrate out of the Bay northward along the Atlantic coast, even as far north as Nova Scotia. There is evidence that most of this ocean-ward migration occurs through the Chesapeake and Delaware Canal, not through the mouth of the Bay.

After the eggs hatch, the young larvae move out of fresh water into the low-salinity waters of upstream nursery areas. As they grow, young stripers gradually move downstream, concentrating along the shoal areas of the Bay and rivers to feed during their first summer. With approaching cold weather, they too move to overwintering grounds in deeper water.

It should be noted that the map shows generalized conditions. In any one season some fish will occur outside the plotted areas.

T. S. Y. K., A. J. L., J. G. B.

Sources: Mansueti and
Hollis (1963); Nichols and Miller (1967).

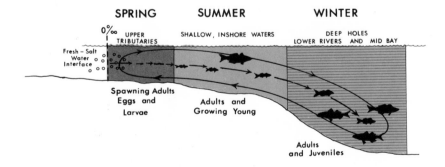

Diagram of the patterns of seasonal movement of various stages in the life of striped bass. Adults and juveniles concentrate in deeper waters in the winter. Adults move to spawning grounds and fresh-saltwater interfaces in the spring, and afterward migrate downstream and tend to concentrate in shallow inshore waters. After hatching, larvae gradually move downstream, spending their first summer in the shallow inshore waters with older juveniles and many adults.

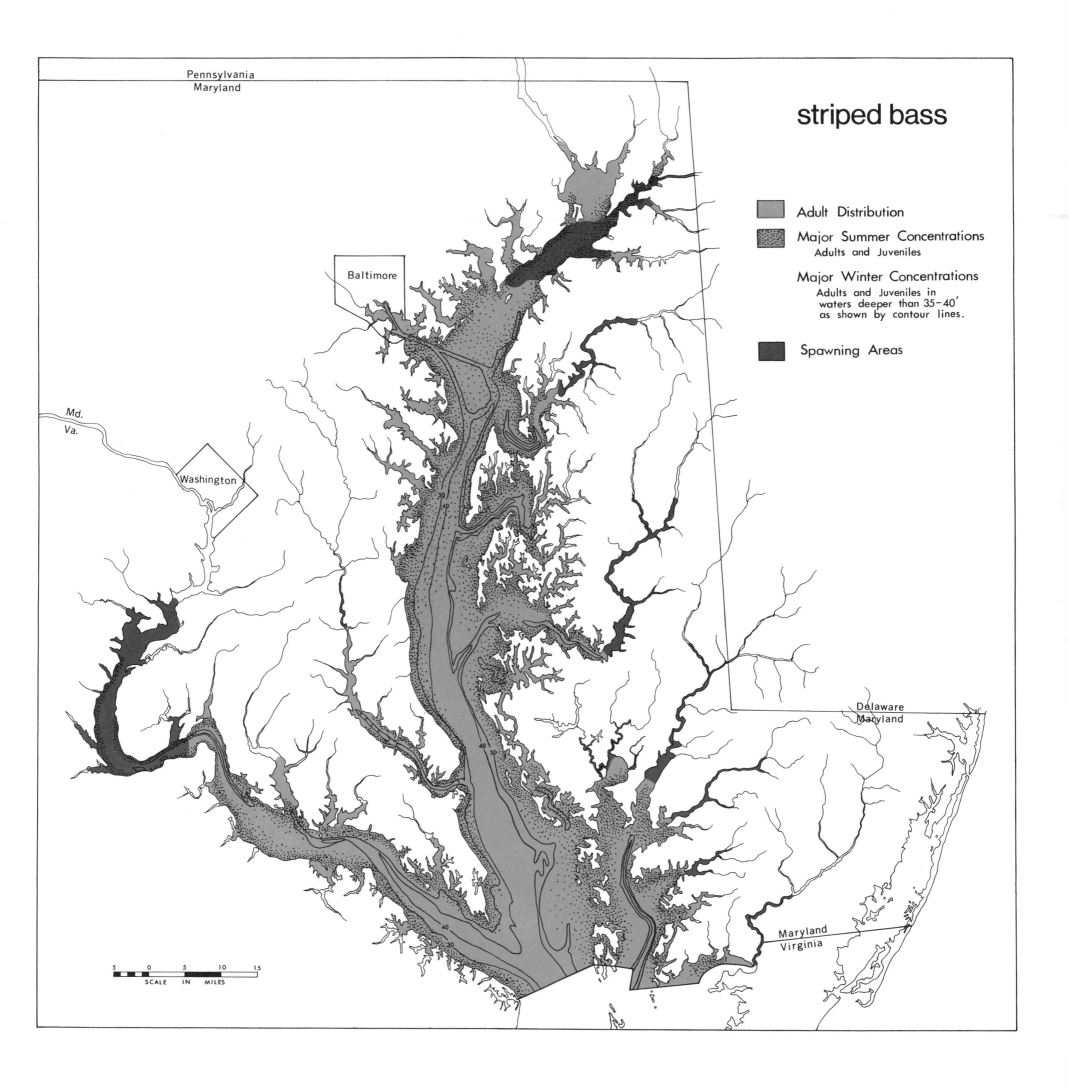

striped bass

Adult Distribution

Major Summer Concentrations
Adults and Juveniles

Major Winter Concentrations
Adults and Juveniles in
waters deeper than 35–40'
as shown by contour lines.

Spawning Areas

Pennsylvania
Maryland

Baltimore

Md.
Va.

Washington

Delaware
Maryland

Maryland
Virginia

5 0 5 10 15
SCALE IN MILES

yellow perch

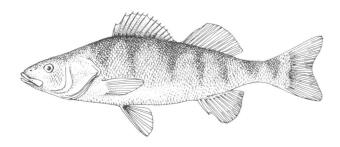

Perca flavescens

Yellow perch are primarily fresh-water fish of lakes and streams, but in the Chesapeake system they are well adapted to estuarine conditions. These common and popular fish are distributed throughout the region in all major tributaries and streams; they tolerate salinities of up to 12 o/oo, but prefer salinities of no more than 7–8 o/oo.

For most of the year, with the exception of the spawning season, they range in the low-salinity portions of each tributary system. From late February to early March, mature adult yellow perch migrate upstream to the spawning grounds at the heads of streams in fresh water. At this time, the dense schools of spawning fish are particularly vulnerable to fishermen. In most cases, the spawning grounds mark the upstream limit of yellow perch distribution in Chesapeake Bay tributaries. In these areas, the easily recognized long, yellow, gelatinous strands of eggs adhere to fallen limbs and other debris.

Spent fish move downstream after spawning to become more scattered in their distribution and less accessible to fishermen. Yellow perch in any stream remain within their particular river system, rarely moving out into the Bay proper. They are not a fish of open deep waters, but prefer more sheltered habitats.

The distribution of yellow perch will vary from that shown on the map according to salinity fluctuations. Their occasional occurrence within the Bay proper has not been mapped. Known spawning areas are marked; some spawning occurs in other suitable areas as well.

M. L. W., R. L. L., A. J. L.

Sources: Mansueti, A. J. (1964);
Hildebrand and Schroeder (1928);
Keup and Bayless (1964);
Whaley and Hopkins (1952);
Mansueti (1960); Muncy (1959).

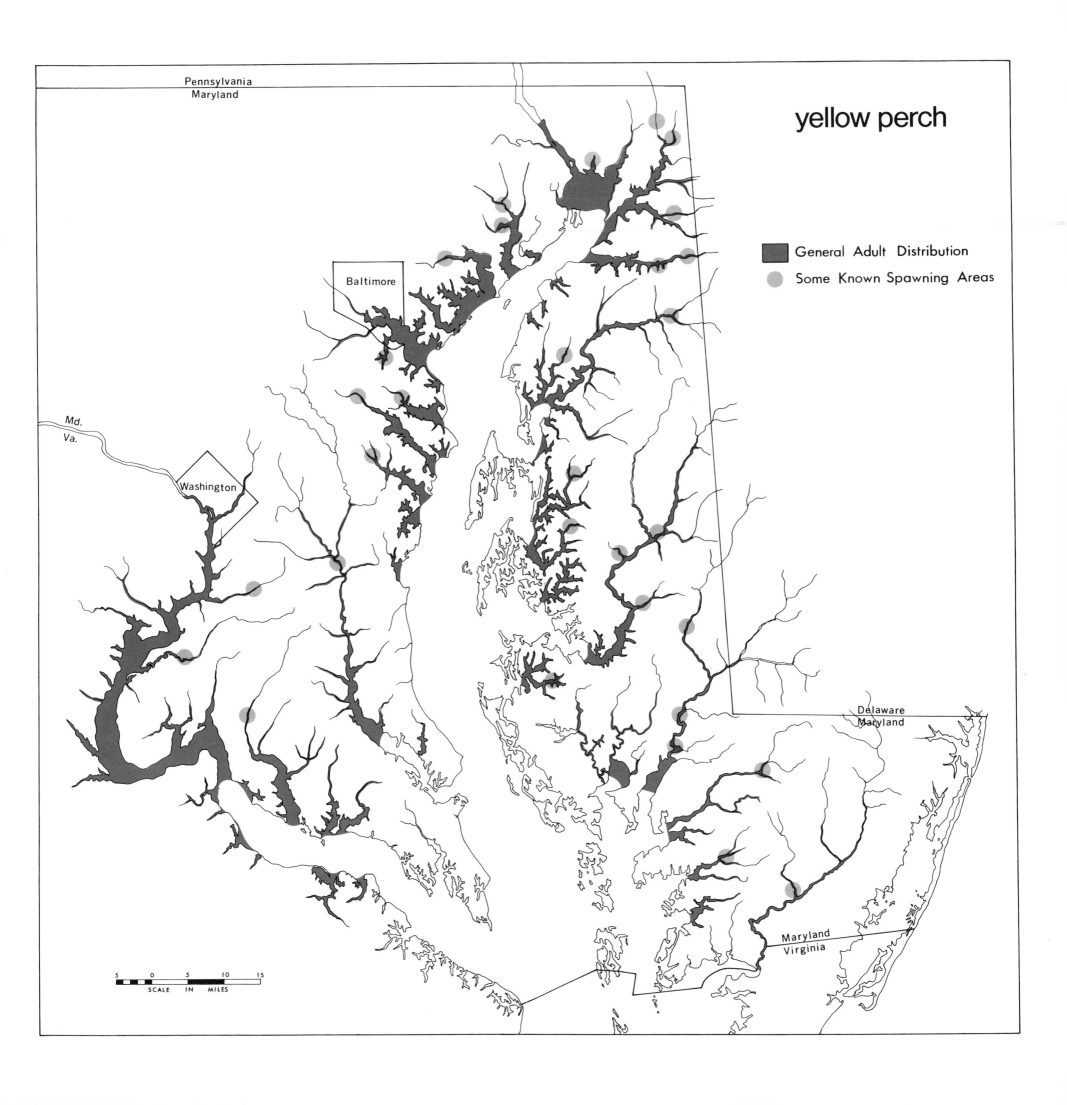

yellow perch

General Adult Distribution
Some Known Spawning Areas

Pennsylvania
Maryland

Baltimore

Md.
Va.

Washington

Delaware
Maryland

Maryland
Virginia

5 0 5 10 15
SCALE IN MILES

bluefish

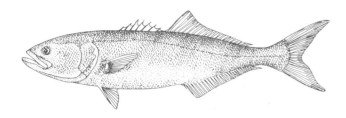

Pomatomus saltatrix

Bluefish are marine fish which enter the Chesapeake Bay in warmer months to feed voraciously on schools of smaller fish, particularly menhaden, anchovies, and silversides. Schools of adult blues, frequently swimming near the surface, usually begin to enter the Bay in March and April. They are found in the Bay throughout the summer and into the fall. The largest catches of bluefish by fishermen are made in September and October. By mid-November, most have returned to the sea, moving offshore and southward. Large adult bluefish are not usually common north of Annapolis. There is great variability in their abundance from year to year. In some years, large numbers of bluefish penetrate far up the Bay; in other years, schools are sparse, with larger bluefish concentrating down-Bay in Virginia waters.

Spawning occurs in the offshore deeper waters of the ocean in early summer. Young-of-the-year, called snappers, move into the Bay in late summer and fall, tending to concentrate in shoal waters. In contrast to adult bluefish, they penetrate much farther up the Bay and its tributaries, where they can be found in water of very low salinity. Many young bluefish apparently enter the upper Bay through the Chesapeake and Delaware Canal.

The range of the bluefish into the Bay's tributaries is not fully documented, but the data that are available permit the general mapping shown here.

M. L. W., J. G. B.

Sources: Hildebrand and Schroeder (1928); Leim and Scott (1966).

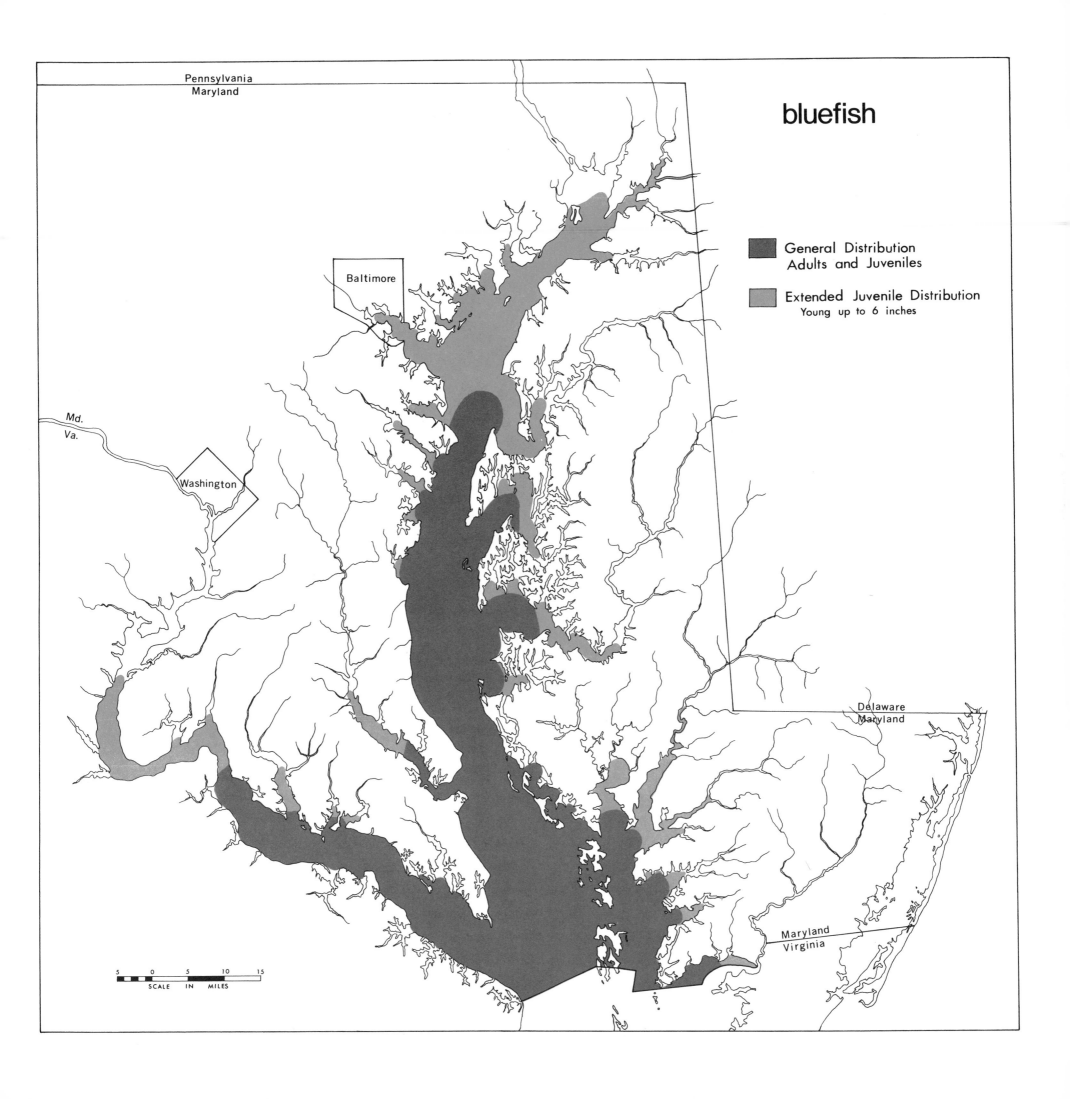

bluefish

■ General Distribution
Adults and Juveniles

■ Extended Juvenile Distribution
Young up to 6 inches

Pennsylvania
Maryland

Baltimore

Md.

Va.

Washington

Delaware
Maryland

Maryland
Virginia

5   0   5   10   15
SCALE   IN   MILES

spot, croaker, and weakfish

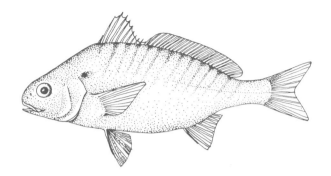

SPOT—*Leiostomus xanthurus*

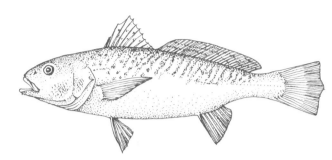

CROAKER, Atlantic Croaker, Hardhead—*Micropogon undulatus*

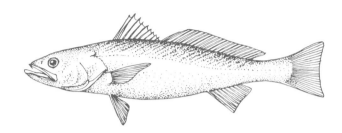

WEAKFISH, Gray Sea Trout, Squeteague—*Cynoscion regalis*

Spot, croaker, and weakfish, closely related species, follow the same distributional patterns, although there are marked differences in their relative abundance. They are principally marine; entering the Chesapeake Bay during warmer months to feed, they return to the sea as cold weather approaches. Their movements are generally toward shore areas in spring and summer, and toward deeper waters as fall approaches. By winter, most have returned to the ocean.

All three species spawn at sea, apparently not far from the mouth of the Bay. After hatching, the larvae and young move into the Bay toward low-salinity, food-rich areas of the upper Bay and its tributaries. Apparently, there is also some movement into the Bay through the Chesapeake and Delaware Canal. As the young fish grow, they tend to move toward deeper and more saline waters. The young fish are thought to spend at least their first year totally in estuarine waters.

The general seasonal movements of these fish are well documented, but the distribution into each individual tributary is not as well known.

Spot

Spot are the most abundant of this group of fishes in the Chesapeake Bay. Their spawning season at sea runs from January through April. Runs of mature adult spot appear in the Bay by early summer, but the heaviest concentrations are found later in the season and into the fall months. Most adults have left the Bay by November. The adults usually do not range as far into low-salinity areas as do the juvenile and immature stages.

Recently hatched young spot enter the Bay in early spring. They follow the generalized pattern of movement that is common to the young of all three species. However, small spot concentrate not only in the major nursery areas upstream (see map) but also inshore along the length of the rivers. Field surveys have documented major nursery areas for spot at the mouth of the Patuxent River and in the upper Bay region between Pooles Island and Turkey Point.

Croaker

Croakers, at one time an abundant Bay species, have become relatively scarce in recent years. Adult croakers enter the Bay in early spring, from March to April, spreading randomly throughout the Bay and the lower reaches of its rivers. However, their range does not extend as far as that of adult spot. As the spawning season approaches, croakers leave the Bay for the ocean; usually all adults have left by the end of October.

The croaker's spawning season is prolonged, extending from August to December. By late summer, the earliest hatched young have already entered the Bay and have begun to migrate to the upper estuaries. This movement of young croakers extends into the late fall and early winter months. Although adult croakers are scarce, young croakers (2–4 inches) can be found in great numbers. Many of them fall prey to predatory striped bass, and cold winters can cause significant mortalities.

Weakfish

Weakfish, which are quite plentiful in the Bay in some years but scarce in others, show a pattern of distribution similar to the croaker, although adult weakfish arrive a little later, from mid-April to the first of May. The spawning season of the two species differs, however; young weakfish utilize the nursery grounds earlier in the season than young croakers. The spawning of weakfish is prolonged, extending from April to August, with the height of activity in May, June, and July. Young weakfish are found moving into and up the Bay by June and July.

Speckled sea trout, *Cynoscion nebulosus*, closely related to weakfish and often confused with them because of their similar appearance, are commonly found in the Chesapeake Bay in the same areas and at the same time as weakfish. They can be distinguished by the numerous black spots over their backs and dorsal fins.

W. L. D., A. J. L.

Sources: Dovel (1971); Welch and Breder (1923); Hildebrand and Schroeder (1928).

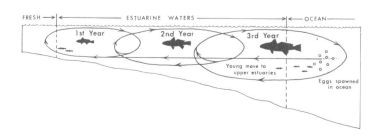

Schematic view of the pattern of distribution of young spot, croaker, and weakfish. Eggs are spawned in the ocean. After hatching, larvae, as they grow, show a generalized movement to upper estuaries. There is a tendency on the part of these fish to remain higher in the estuaries in their first year, gradually to extend their downstream range, and to limit their upstream range as they grow older.

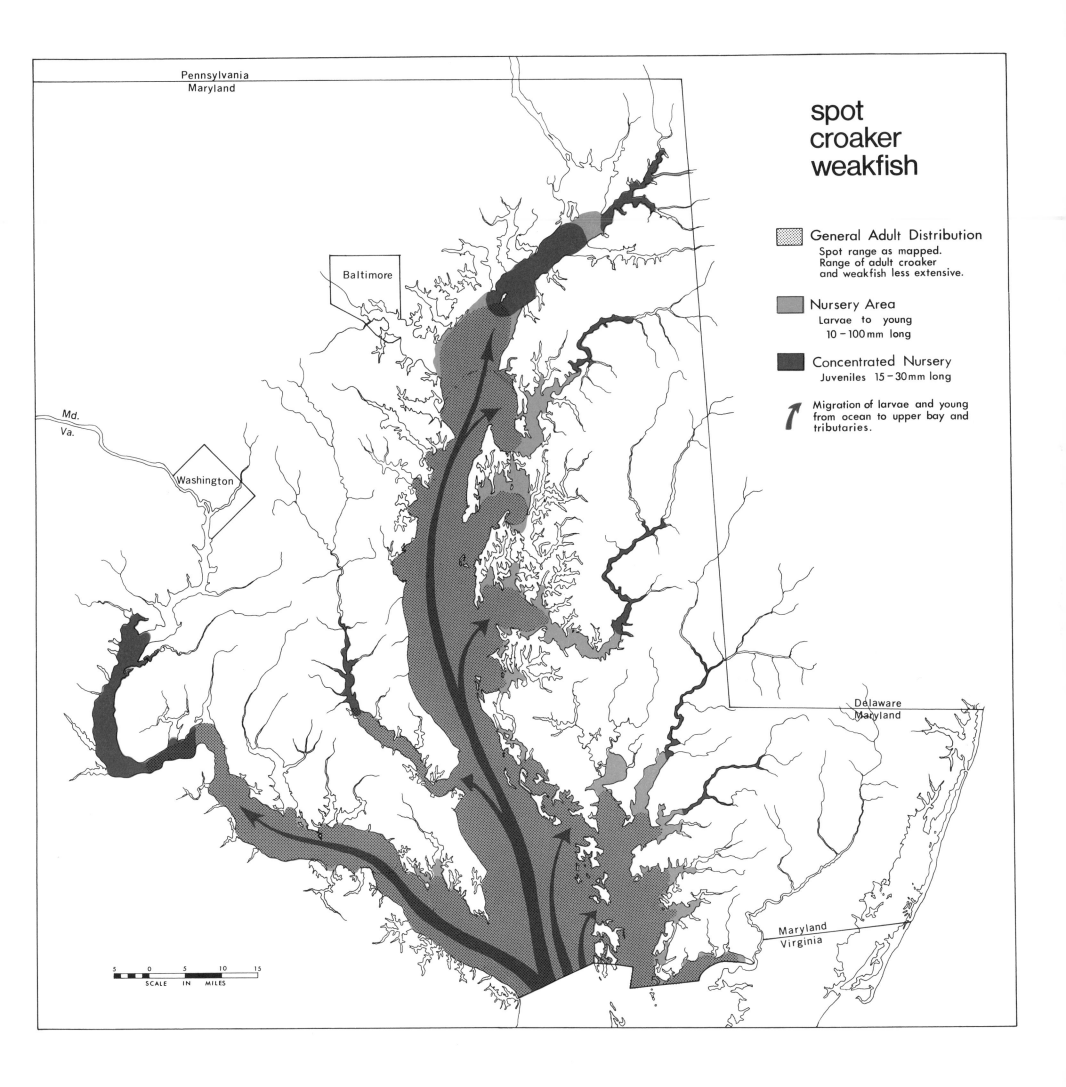

spot
croaker
weakfish

General Adult Distribution
Spot range as mapped.
Range of adult croaker
and weakfish less extensive.

Nursery Area
Larvae to young
10 – 100 mm long

Concentrated Nursery
Juveniles 15 – 30 mm long

Migration of larvae and young
from ocean to upper bay and
tributaries.

Pennsylvania
Maryland

Baltimore

Md.
Va.

Washington

Delaware
Maryland

Maryland
Virginia

5   0   5   10   15
SCALE   IN   MILES

atlantic silverside and northern puffer

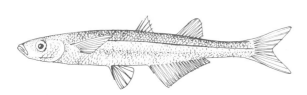

SILVERSIDE—*Menidia menidia*

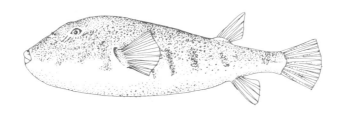

PUFFER, Swellfish, Sea Squab—*Spheroides maculatus*

Atlantic Silverside

The Atlantic silverside, an extremely common and abundant species, occurs in large schools throughout the Bay region, even into fresh water. An important forage fish for many predators, it is matched or exceeded in abundance in the Chesapeake Bay only by the bay anchovy, *Anchoa mitchilli*. The Atlantic silverside is essentially a fish of inshore shoal areas; it prefers tidal creeks with grass flats, although it moves to deeper channel waters in winter. The Atlantic silverside spawns in shallow waters in May, and the adhesive eggs attach to suitable substrate. Larvae and young are abundant in lower-salinity waters (1–15 o/oo).

The tidewater silverside, *Menidia beryllina,* and the rough silverside, *Membras membras,* both of which closely resemble the Atlantic silverside, also occur in the Chesapeake Bay.

The tidewater silverside is usually found in areas of lower salinity than the Atlantic silverside, and may enter fresh water, which the Atlantic silverside rarely does. The rough silverside and Atlantic silverside generally have similar distributions within the Bay proper, but there is some question as to the distribution of the Atlantic silverside into the Susquehanna Flats. The tidewater silverside definitely is found there.

Northern Puffer

Puffers inhabit the lower portion of Maryland's Chesapeake Bay area and are most heavily concentrated along the Eastern Shore. Puffers are unique because of their ability to swell into ball-like shapes at will. For many years they were not harvested, but recently, due to a new appreciation for the quality of their flesh, a fishery has been established in the lower part of the Maryland portion of the Bay and in the Tangier Sound area. However, rapid population fluctuations from year to year create significant problems for fishermen.

Puffers are widely distributed in Virginia and lower Maryland waters from April to November, but apparently most move out of the Bay in winter. Spawning occurs in May in shoal areas. The small, highly adhesive eggs are attached to the substrate. Larvae and young (from 1.7 to 2.0 millimeters and longer) have been found from May to September in deeper areas throughout the broad region of the puffer's distribution in Maryland. Puffers can tolerate salinities as low as 9 o/oo, so there is some infrequent occurrence up-Bay as well. Records on puffers are not sufficient to establish the extent of their movement up the Bay's tributaries.

M. L. W., R. L. L., W. R. C.

Sources: Shipp and Yerger (1969); Hildebrand and Schroeder (1928); Bayliffe (1950); Leim and Scott (1966) on the silverside.

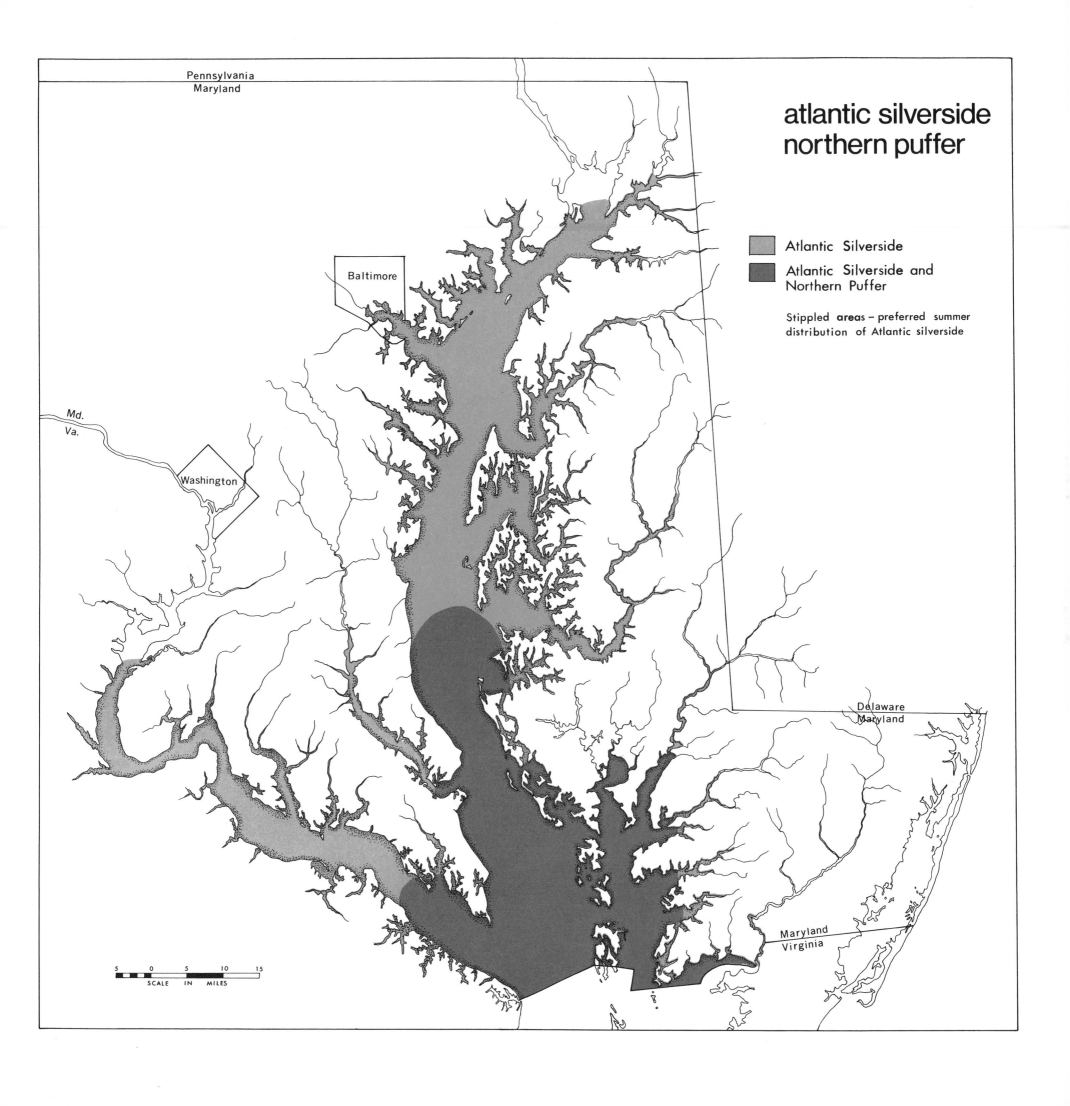

atlantic silverside
northern puffer

Atlantic Silverside

Atlantic Silverside and
Northern Puffer

Stippled areas – preferred summer
distribution of Atlantic silverside

Pennsylvania
Maryland

Baltimore

Md.
Va.

Washington

Delaware
Maryland

Maryland
Virginia

5   0   5   10   15
SCALE   IN   MILES

winter flounder

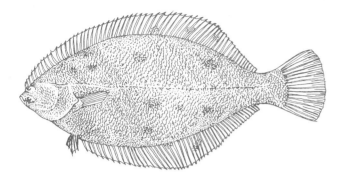

Pseudopleuronectes americanus

Winter flounder are common winter residents of Maryland's portion of the Chesapeake Bay. Although they are primarily ocean fish, these bottom-dwelling flatfish are widely distributed throughout the Bay and many of its tributaries into lower-salinity waters. They are found up-Bay at least to the Sassafras River. The area of greatest concentration in Maryland tends to be the open Bay between Kent Island and Hooper Island, particularly along the Eastern Shore.

Individual winter flounder enter the Chesapeake Bay to feed and spawn during the winter months and migrate back to sea during the summer months. Winter flounder are cold-water fish and apparently do not tolerate the higher summer temperatures of Bay waters. This seasonal pattern contrasts with that of many other migrant fish species which enter the Bay in spring or early summer and leave with the onset of winter. Summer flounder, *Paralichthys dentatus,* the only other large flatfish common to Maryland waters, follow this more general pattern.

Winter flounder are present mostly from November through May, being practically absent from June to October. These fish prefer deeper channel waters, but move into the mouths of rivers and to shallower water to spawn. Spawning occurs from mid-February to mid-March, when water temperatures range from 0.0 to 5.6°C. Eggs sink to the bottom, cling together, and are virtually unaffected by currents; consequently, they are not transported from the spawning grounds like the light, buoyant eggs of many other species. Juveniles apparently remain within the Bay and its lower tributaries in shallow, inshore waters during their first summer.

The spawning areas plotted on the map are areas in which spawning has been documented; however, spawning probably occurs in other areas as well.

T. S. Y. K.

Sources: Koo (1966, 1967); Perlmutter (1946).

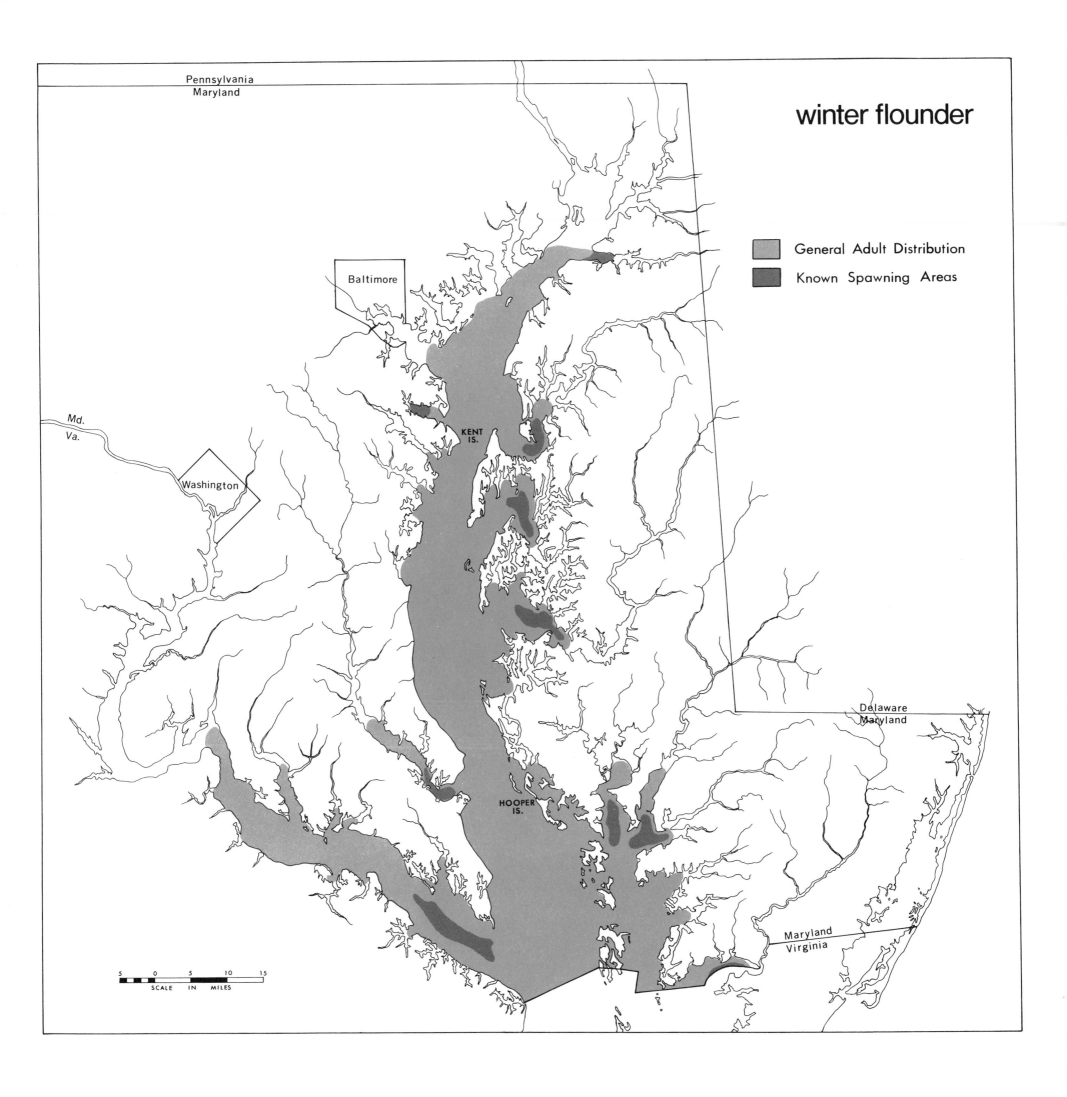

winter flounder

General Adult Distribution

Known Spawning Areas

Pennsylvania
Maryland

Baltimore

Md.
Va.

Washington

KENT
IS.

Delaware
Maryland

HOOPER
IS.

Maryland
Virginia

5   0   5   10   15
SCALE   IN   MILES

hogchoker and bay anchovy

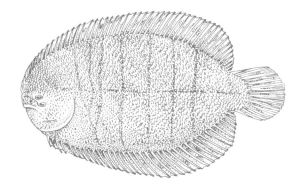

HOGCHOKER—*Trinectes maculatus*

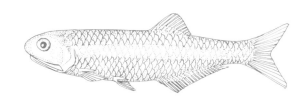

BAY ANCHOVY, Anchovy—*Anchoa mitchilli*

These two species are members of quite different families of fishes, but they are grouped together here because of the similarity in their distributional patterns. Both the hogchoker and the Bay anchovy are ubiquitous but unharvested estuarine fish. They both have extended summer spawning periods in the same general areas; the larvae of both migrate to low-salinity, upstream nursery regions; the larger adults of both species tend to concentrate downstream; and both species exhibit some distribution far into fresh water.

Hogchoker

Hogchokers are well-adapted and abundant estuarine fish which range from marine waters to fresh water. Some small adults, two and three years old, will on occasion travel 40–50 miles into fresh water. In spite of their great abundance, no fishery exists for these small bottom-feeding flatfish (maximum length, 8 inches). The adult population is generally found in higher salinities, while juveniles tend to concentrate in lower salinities. There is some evidence that discrete hogchoker populations occur in various Bay tributaries. A predictable seasonal migration is apparent, with spawning populations moving toward higher-salinity waters in the spring.

The extensive spawning grounds of the hogchoker are located in the lower reaches of rivers and in the Bay in salinities greater than about 9 o/oo, although some eggs have been found in lower salinities. The spawning season extends from May to September and peaks in July and August. During the first year, young hogchokers tend to remain in primary nursery areas, with salinities of less than 10 o/oo, but, with each successive spring and summer migration, the young fish descend farther down the rivers (see diagram).

Bay Anchovy

Bay anchovies are one of the most abundant species of fish in the Chesapeake Bay. They are small fish that move in large schools, and are an important forage species for many predators. Anchovies have been found to be a major portion of the diet of striped bass. Related species of anchovies are harvested in various parts of the world as food fish, but no commercial fishery exists in the Chesapeake Bay.

The Bay anchovy is a resident species found in all parts of the Bay and its tributaries, even into fresh water. Certain migratory patterns within the estuarine system can be ascertained for various stages. Spawning occurs over a wide salinity range, but peak spawning is in the range of 13–15 o/oo. The spawning season is protracted, running from late April into September, but the greatest numbers of eggs are produced in July and August. Recently hatched larvae apparently congregate in rich, low-salinity areas near the salt-water/fresh-water interface up the rivers and in the upper reaches of the Chesapeake Bay. Many young-of-the-year remain in these primary nursery areas at least through their first summer. Schools of adults are randomly distributed throughout the estuary in warmer months, and are more concentrated in deeper waters and lower down the tributaries during the winter months.

W. L. D., M. L. W.

Sources: Dovel et al. (1969);
Hildebrand and Schroeder (1928); Daly (1970); Dovel (1971).

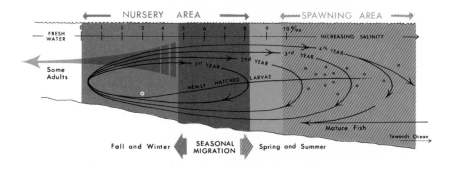

Schematic diagram showing patterns of movements of life-history stages of the hogchoker. Newly hatched larvae move upstream to a rich nursery area where they spend their first few months. With the onset of their first spring, they tend to move downstream with spawning adults, but they do not travel as far. In the fall, they move back upstream. With each year of growth, there is a decreasing tendency to move upstream in late summer, but an increasing tendency to move farther downstream in the spring. After about their fourth year, their movements appear to be more random.

Anchovies display a similar pattern of movement, at least through their first year.

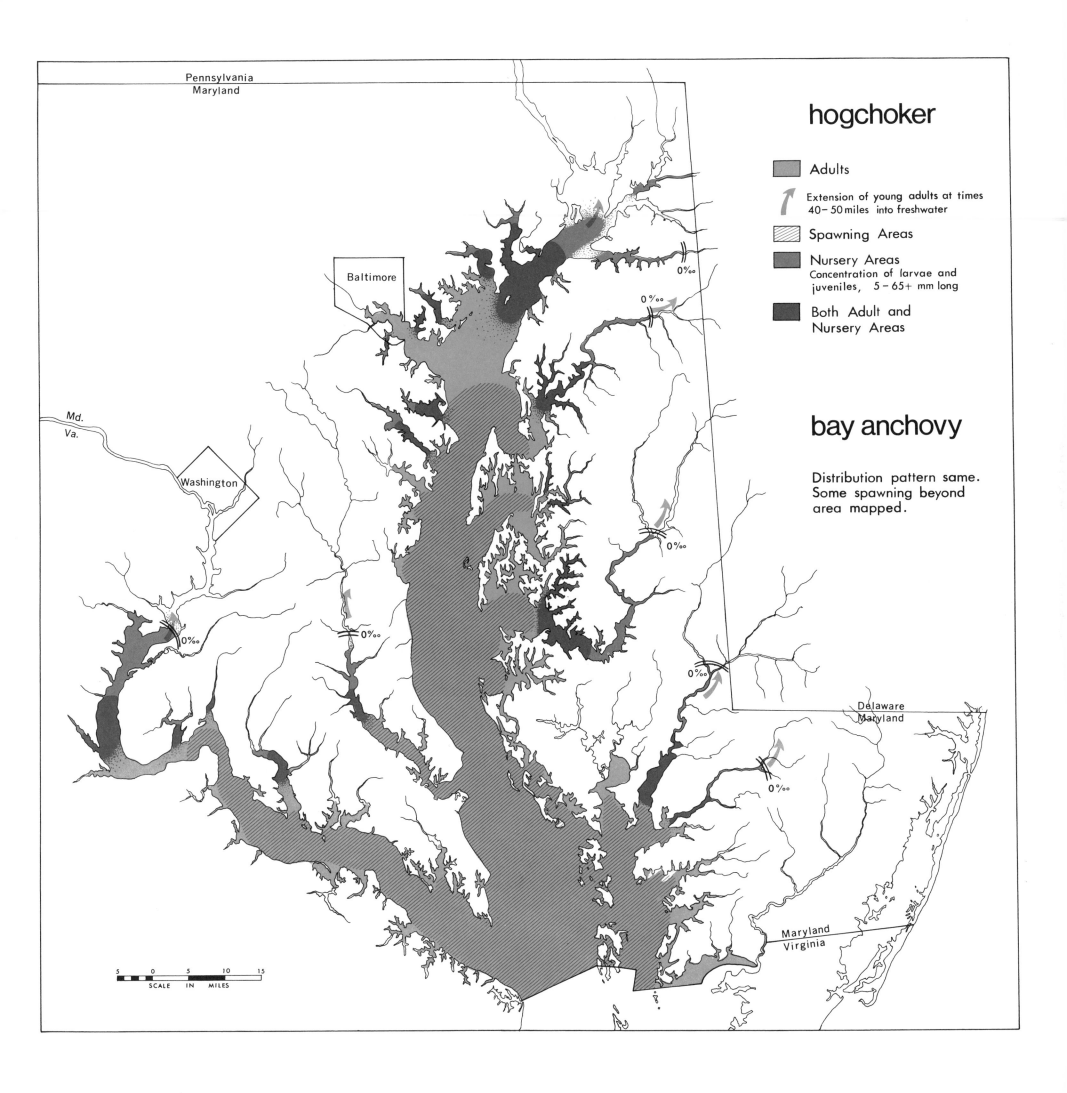

hogchoker

- Adults
- Extension of young adults at times 40–50 miles into freshwater
- Spawning Areas
- Nursery Areas
  Concentration of larvae and juveniles, 5–65+ mm long
- Both Adult and Nursery Areas

bay anchovy

Distribution pattern same. Some spawning beyond area mapped.

Pennsylvania
Maryland

Baltimore

Md.
Va.

Washington

0‰

0‰

0‰

0‰

0‰

0‰

0‰

Delaware
Maryland

Maryland
Virginia

SCALE IN MILES
5 0 5 10 15

ducks

DABBLING DUCKS

1. Mallard—*Anas platyrhynchos*
2. Black Duck—*Anas rubripes*
3. Wood Duck—*Aix sponsa*

OTHER COMMON DABBLERS

Pintail, *Anas acuta*; Gadwall, *Anas strepera*; American Widgeon (Baldpate), *Mareca americana*; Shoveler, *Spatula clypeata*; Blue-Winged Teal, *Anas discors*; and Green-Winged Teal, *Anas carolinensis*.

DIVING DUCKS

4. Lesser Scaup—*Aythya affinis*
5. Canvasback—*Aythya valisineria*

OTHER COMMON DIVERS

Greater Scaup, *Aythya marila*; Ring-Necked Duck, *Aythya collaris*; Common Goldeneye, *Bucephala clangula*; Bufflehead, *Bucephala albeola*; Ruddy Duck, *Oxyura jamaicensis*; Common Eider, *Somateria mollissima*; Common

6. Oldsquaw—*Clangula hyemalis*
7. Redhead—*Aythya americana*
8. Surf Scoter—*Melanitta perspicillata*

Scoter, *Oidemia nigra*; White-Winged Scoter, *Melanitta deglandi*; Common Merganser, *Mergus merganser*; Red-Breasted Merganser, *Merganser serrator*; and Hooded Merganser, *Lophodytes cucullatus*.

Dabblers

Dabblers usually tip to feed in shallow water and spring aloft when flushing; their legs are more centered along the body axis; the hind toe is unlobed; their wing surface is relatively large in relation to body volume; most have an iridescent rectangle of color on the wing (a speculum); and they have brown eyes.

Divers

Divers dive to feed in waters from 1 foot to over 100 feet deep and patter across the water to get awing; their legs are placed posteriorly, which makes them awkward walkers on land; the hind toe is lobed; their wing surface is less than that of dabblers in relation to body volume; obscure or no iridescent colors are found on the wing surface; and many divers have red, yellow, or white eyes.

Wherever there is water in Maryland, a duck can be found at some time during the year. The vast majority of our ducks are produced in Canada,

but a few thousand nest here, particularly black ducks and wood ducks.

The most numerous and widespread wintering dabblers in Maryland are mallards (closely associated with harvested cornfields) and black ducks (common in marshes and swamps).

Lesser scaup, old squaws, surf scoters, and white-winged scoters are the most abundant ducks in Maryland. The scaup often number in the hundreds of thousands in the Potomac River and on the Calvert County Bay shore, and at other times they are widely scattered throughout the tidewater region. The sea ducks listed (oldsquaw and scoters) number in the hundreds of thousands, primarily on deeper waters, where they are usually unobserved by the layman. The number of sea ducks included on the accompanying map reflects only those noted within one-half to three-quarters of a mile of the shoreline.

The Chesapeake's most noteworthy duck is the canvasback, whose number has been drastically reduced since the mid-1950s, due primarily to habitat conditions on the breeding grounds in the prairie provinces of Canada. Where once the canvasback was widely found wintering in large rafts along most Chesapeake Bay shorelines, it is now

found in relatively large concentrations only along the central Potomac River, Calvert County shorelines, Kent County shorelines, the lower Choptank River, and the Honga River–Fishing Bay–lower Nanticoke River section.

The distribution and abundance of ducks at any one point is reflected by the condition of the habitat. The condition of some of the Chesapeake Bay duck habitat shows insidious deterioration, due primarily to reduced light penetration, which is necessary for good production of submerged, native food plants.

The number and distribution of ducks are affected by conditions of the migration or wintering habitat in Maryland and elsewhere and of the nesting habitat in Canada, as well as by the vagaries of weather. Consequently, gross annual changes in the number and distribution of ducks are commonplace on the Chesapeake Bay. Surveys determine only minimal estimates because of the problems of sighting the ducks in many areas and the impossibility of surveying all possible duck habitats.

V. D. S.

Sources: Robbins *et al.* (1966); Stewart (1962); Stewart and Robbins (1958); Linduska *et al.* (1964); Kortright (1943); Hochbaum (1955).

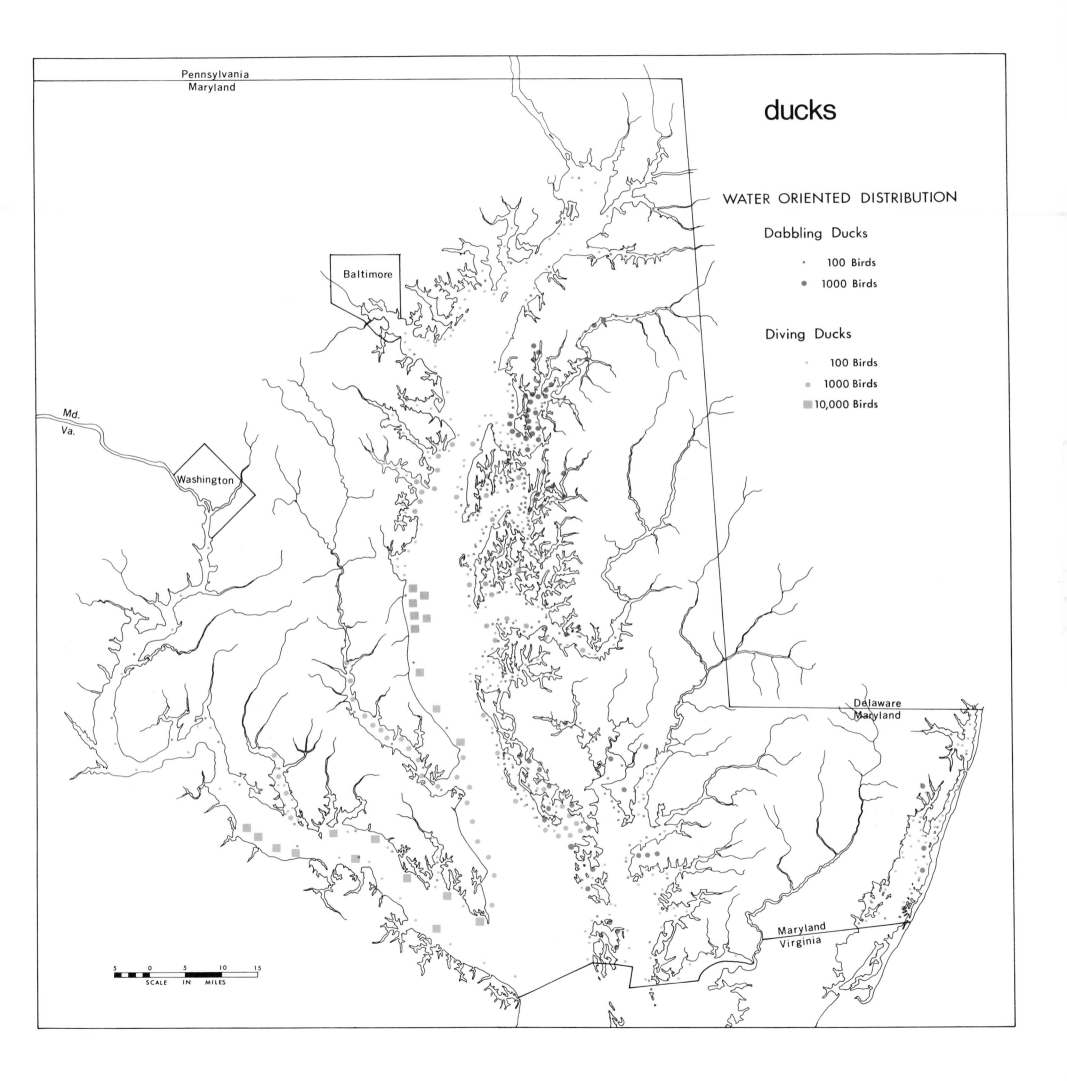

ducks

WATER ORIENTED DISTRIBUTION

Dabbling Ducks

· 100 Birds

● 1000 Birds

Diving Ducks

· 100 Birds

● 1000 Birds

■ 10,000 Birds

geese and swans

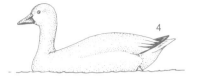

1. Canada Goose—*Branta canadensis*
2. Brant—*Branta bernicla*
3. Greater Snow Goose—*Chen hyperborea atlanticus*
   Lesser Snow Goose—*Chen hyperborea subsp.*
   (similar in appearance to *Chen hyperborea atlanticus*)
4. Whistling Swan—*Olor columbianus*

Migrating south for the winter season, vast hordes of geese and swans settle in the Chesapeake Bay region, with the greatest concentration of flocks occurring along the Eastern Shore tributaries (see map). Canada geese start arriving by the end of September. The other species begin to appear the first part of October. Spring migration away from the area begins by the end of February or the first of March, and most birds are gone by the end of April. Except for mute swans, which are reared locally and northward into lower New England, the Chesapeake's wintering geese and swans are produced in the Arctic regions of Canada and Alaska.

Our most numerous migrational-wintering waterfowl is the Canada goose, which usually numbers a half-million or more annually. Geese are primarily grazers and are well adapted to walking on land and springing into the air when disturbed. Their primary habitats here are the large cereal grainfields bordering tidewater between the Bohemia and Choptank Rivers. Canada geese and lesser snow geese readily adapted to cornfield grazing in the 1940s with the advent of the mechanical cornpicker, which left much waste grain. Farm ponds and other water impoundments have become important concentration centers. Waste corn, a high energy food, is necessary for physical maintenance during prolonged cold weather. Otherwise, Canada

geese feed primarily on green grain crops, green broadleaved weeds and grasses, submerged aquatic grasses, and emergent marsh plant stems and roots. Canada geese are taxonomically subdivided into about a dozen races, ranging in size from the giant Canada goose to the cackling goose. Several races winter in the Chesapeake.

Lesser snow geese accompany Canada geese in field-feeding. Greater snow geese, normally grazers on emergent marsh plant stems and root stalks of the marshes of the ocean bays, are now beginning to field-feed. Blue geese have recently been lumped with lesser snow geese into one subspecies, since recent observations showed that both types are produced from the same nest.

Brant are more marine-oriented than most of the waterfowl species; they continue to feed in shoal-water habitats, mostly on rooted grasses and algae. Their primary wintering distribution is along the ocean bays, with lesser numbers on the Eastern Shore bayfront below the Little Choptank River.

Whistling swans, which are more awkward on land than geese, have been most common in the extensive shoal-water areas of the Choptank and Chester Rivers. However, a major exodus from shoal-water feeding to field-feeding began during the winter of 1969/70, when six weeks of ice prevented normal feeding habits.

Deterioration of submerged plant beds in recent years also probably contributed significantly to the recent field-feeding tendencies which are now common between the Sassafras and Nanticoke Rivers.

Breeding mute swans (*Cynus dor*), now in the order of 75–100 birds, are found primarily in the Miles and Tred Avon Rivers. The probable Chesapeake wintering population totals about 100–200 birds, mostly in water habitats frequented by whistling swans. They can be considered an undesirable species, since they are extremely antagonistic to whistling swans and geese and oftentimes keep other waterfowl from utilizing available habitats for food and cover.

Geese and swans are less affected by nesting conditions than ducks. Conditions of migration or wintering habitat and the weather have had minor annual effects, but major long-term effects, in the distribution and numbers of these species. Survey data for geese and swans are far more reliable and consistent than those for ducks; geese can be seen more easily, and their habitats are less difficult to survey.

V. D. S.

Sources: Robbins *et al.* (1966); Stewart (1962); Stewart and Robbins (1958); Linduska *et al.* 1964); Kortright (1943); Hochbaum (1955); Hine *et al.* (1968).

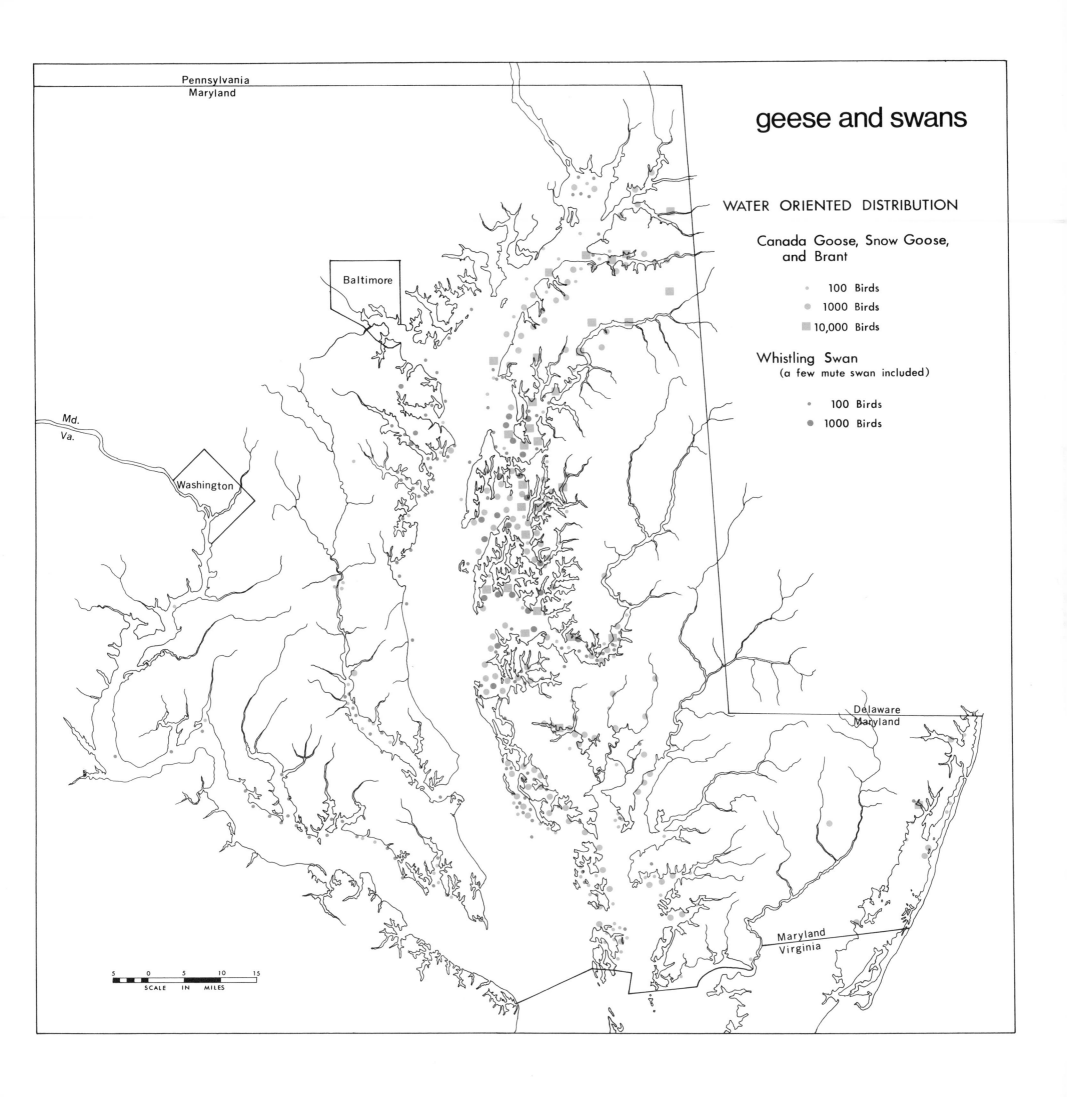

geese and swans

WATER ORIENTED DISTRIBUTION

Canada Goose, Snow Goose, and Brant

·   100 Birds

●   1000 Birds

■   10,000 Birds

Whistling Swan
(a few mute swan included)

·   100 Birds

●   1000 Birds

Pennsylvania
Maryland

Baltimore

Md.
Va.

Washington

Delaware
Maryland

Maryland
Virginia

5 0 5 10 15
SCALE IN MILES

bibliography

Books

Bertin, L. 1956. *Eels: A Biological Study*. London, Cleaver-Hume Press.

Hine, R. L., *et al.* 1968. *Canada Goose Management: Current Continental Problems and Programs*. Dembar Educational Research Services.

Hochbaum, H. A. 1955. *Travels and Traditions of Waterfowl*. Minneapolis, University of Minnesota Press.

Kortright, F. H. 1943. *The Ducks, Geese, and Swans of North America*. Washington, D.C., American Wildlife Institute.

Linduska, J. P., *et al.* 1964. *Waterfowls Tomorrow*. Washington, D.C., U.S. Department of the Interior.

Mansueti, A. J., and Hardy, J. D. 1967. *Development of Fishes of the Chesapeake Bay Region: An Atlas of Egg, Larval, and Juvenile Stages*, pt. 1. Natural Resources Institute, University of Maryland.

Robbins, C. S., *et al.* 1966. *A Guide to Field Identification of Birds of North America*. New York, Golden Press.

Spinner, G. P. 1969. *The Wildlife Wetlands and Shellfish Areas of the Atlantic Coastal Zone*. Serial Atlas of the Marine Environment, folio 18. American Geographic Society.

Stewart, R. E., and Robbins, C. S. 1958. *Birds of Maryland and the District of Columbia*. U.S. Department of the Interior, North American Fauna, no. 62.

Journal Articles

Bigelow, H. B., and Shroeder, W. C. 1953. "Fishes of the Gulf of Maine." *Bulletin of the U.S. Bureau of Fisheries*, no. 74.

Bishop, J. W. 1972. "Ctenophores of the Chesapeake Bay." *Chesapeake Science*, 13, suppl.: S98–S100.

Churchill, E. P. 1919. "Life History of the Blue Crab." *Bulletin of the U.S. Bureau of Fisheries*, no. 36.

Cronin, L. E. 1967. "The Condition of the Chesapeake Bay." *Transactions of the Thirty-second North American Wildlife and Natural Resources Conference*. Wildlife Management Institute.

Daly, R. J. 1970. "Systematics of Southern Florida Anchovies (Pisces: Engraulidae)." *Bulletin of Marine Science*, 20, no. 1: 70–104.

Dovel, W. L.; Mihursky, J. A.; and McErlean, A. J. 1969. "Life History Aspects of the Hogchoker, *Trinectes maculatus*, in the Patuxent River Estuary, Maryland." *Chesapeake Science*, 10, no. 2: 104–19.

Flemer, D. A. 1970. "Primary Production in the Chesapeake Bay." *Chesapeake Science*, 11, no. 2: 117–29.

Hildebrand, S. F., and Schroeder, W. C. 1928. "Fishes of Chesapeake Bay." *Bulletin of the U.S. Bureau of Fisheries*, no. 43.

Keup, L., and Bayless, J. 1964. "Fish Distribution at Varying Salinities in Neuse River Basin, North Carolina." *Chesapeake Science*, 5, no. 3: 119–23.

Mansueti, A. J. 1964. "Early Development of the Yellow Perch, *Perca flavescens*." *Chesapeake Science*, 5, nos. 1–2: 46–66.

Mansueti, R. J. 1960. "Comparison of the Movements of Stocked and Resident Yellow Perch, *Perca flavescens*, in Tributaries of Chesapeake Bay, Maryland." *Chesapeake Science*, 3, no. 1: 21–35.

————. 1961. "Movements, Reproduction, and Mortality of the White Perch, *Roccus americanus*, in the Patuxent Estuary, Maryland." *Chesapeake Science*, 2, nos. 3–4: 142–205.

————. 1964. "Eggs, Larvae, and Young of the White Perch, *Roccus americanus*, with Comments on Its Ecology in the Estuary." *Chesapeake Science*, 5, nos. 1–2: 3–45.

Nichols, P. R., and Miller, R. V. 1967. "Seasonal Movements of Striped Bass, *Roccus saxatilis* (Walbaum), Tagged and Released in the Potomac River, Maryland, 1959–61." *Chesapeake Science*, 8, no. 2: 102–24.

Perlmutter, A. 1946. "The Distribution of the Winter Flounder, *Pseudopleuronectes americanus*, and Its Bearing on Management Possibilities." *Transactions of the Eleventh North American Wildlife Conferences*, pp. 239–50. Wildlife Management Institute.

Pfitzenmeyer, H. T., and Drobeck, K. G. 1964. "The Occurrence of the Brackish-Water Clam, *Rangia cuneata*, in the Potomac River, Maryland." *Chesapeake Science*, 5, no. 4: 209–12.

Pritchard, D. W. 1952. "Salinity Distribution and Circulation in the Chesapeake Bay Estuarine System." *Journal of Marine Research*, 2, no. 2: 106–23.

Shipp, R. L., and Yerger, R. W. 1969. "Status, Characters, and Distribution of the Northern and Southern Puffers of the Genus *Spheroides*." *Copeia*, no. 3, pp. 425–33.

Sieling, F. W. 1956. "The Hard-Shell Clam Fishery of Maryland Waters." *Maryland Tidewater News*, 12, no. 10, suppl. 9.

Van Engel, W. A. 1958. "The Blue Crab and Its Fishery in Chesapeake Bay, Part 1." U.S. Fish and Wildlife Service, *Commercial Fisheries Review*, 20, no. 6.

Welch, W. W., and Breder, C. M. 1923. "Contributions to Life Histories of Scianidae of the Eastern U.S. Coast." *Bulletin of the U.S. Bureau of Fisheries*, no. 39, pp. 141–201.

Pamphlets and Reports

Bayliff, W. H., Jr. 1950. *The Life History of the Silverside,* Menidia menidia (*Linnaeus*). Chesapeake Biological Laboratory, Publication no. 90.

Biggs, R. B. 1970. "Gross Physical and Biological Effects of Overboard Spoil Disposal in Upper Chesapeake Bay, Project A: Final Report to the Bureau of Sport Fisheries and Wildlife." Natural Resources Institute, University of Maryland, Special Report no. 3.

Bosch, H. F., and Taylor, W. R. 1970. "Ecology of *Podon polyphemoides* (Crustacae, Brancipoda) in the Chesapeake Bay." Chesapeake Bay Institute, The Johns Hopkins University, Technical Report no. 66.

Carriker, M. E. 1955. "Critical Review of Biology and Control of Oyster Drills, *Urosalpinx* and *Eupleura*." U.S. Fish and Wildlife Service, Special Scientific Report, Fish, no. 148.

Cronin, W. B. 1971. "Volumetric, Areal, and Tidal Statistics of the Chesapeake Bay Estuary and Its Tributaries." Chesapeake Bay Institute, The Johns Hopkins University, Special Report no. 20.

Dovel, W. L. 1971. "Fish Eggs and Larvae of the Upper Chesapeake Bay." Natural Resources Institute, University of Maryland, Special Report no. 4.

Eales, J. G. 1967. "A Bibliography of the Eels of the Genus *Anguilla*." Fisheries Research Board of Canada, Technical Report no. 28.

Frey, D. G. 1946. "Oyster Bars of the Potomac River." U.S. Fish and Wildlife Service, Special Scientific Report no. 32.

Goodwin, F., Jr. 1968. "Zooplankton." In *Biological and Geological Research on the Effects of Dredging and Spoil Disposal in the Upper Chesapeake Bay*. Eighth Progress Report, Natural Resources Institute, University of Maryland, Reference no. 68-2B.

Heinle, D. R. 1969. "Effects of Temperature on the Population Dynamics of Estuarine Copepods." Ph.D. thesis, University of Maryland.

Koo, T. S. Y. 1966. "Commercial Fisheries Research and Development Act: Final Report for Contract Year Ending 31 August 1966." Natural Resources Institute, University of Maryland, Reference no. 66-19-C.

———. 1967. "Commercial Fisheries Research and Development Act: Final Report for Contract Year Ending 31 August 1967." Natural Resources Institute, University of Maryland, Reference no. 67-6-C.

Leim, A. H., and Scott, W. B. 1966. *Fishes of the Atlantic Coast of Canada*. Fisheries Research Board of Canada, Bulletin no. 155.

Lippson, R. L. 1971. "Blue Crab Study in Chesapeake Bay, Maryland." Natural Resources Institute, University of Maryland, Annual Progress Report no. 71-9.

Mansueti, R. J., and Hollis, E. H. 1963. "Striped Bass in Maryland Tidewaters." Natural Resources Institute, University of Maryland, Educational Series, no. 61.

Metzgar, R. G. 1972. *Wetlands in Maryland*. Maryland Department of State Planning, Baltimore, Maryland, Publication no. 157.

Muncy, R. J. 1959. "Evaluation of the Yellow Perch Hatchery Program in Maryland." Maryland Department of Research and Education, Solomons, Maryland, Resource Study Report no. 15.

Pritchard, D. W. 1966. "A Preliminary Estimate of the Effect of Diversion of Flow from the Susquehanna River on the Salinity of the Upper Chesapeake Bay." Eleventh Coordinating Committee Meeting of the Susquehanna River Basin Study, October 4, 1966.

Ryan, J. D. 1953. *The Sediments of Chesapeake Bay*. Maryland Board of Natural Resources, Department of Geology, Mines, and Water Resources, Bulletin no. 12.

Schultz, L. P., and Cargo, D. G. 1971. "The Sea Nettle of Chesapeake Bay." Natural Resources Institute, University of Maryland, Educational Series, no. 93.

Stewart, R. E. 1962. "Waterfowl Populations in the Upper Chesapeake Region." U.S. Department of the Interior, Fish and Wildlife Service, Bureau of Sports Fisheries and Wildlife, Special Scientific Report, Wildlife, no. 65.

Truitt, R. V. 1939. "The Blue Crab of the Chesapeake Bay." In *Our Water Resources and Their Conservation*. Chesapeake Biological Laboratory, Solomons, Maryland, Contribution no. 27.

U.S. Department of Commerce, Coast and Geodetic Survey. 1930. *Tides and Currents in Chesapeake Bay and Tributaries*. Special Publication no. 162.

———. 1961. *Natural Oyster Bar Charts of Maryland*. Prepared for the Maryland Department of Tidewater Fisheries.

Whaley, H. H., and Hopkins, T. C. 1952. "Graphical Summary Report No. I: Atlas of the Salinity and Temperature Distribution of Chesapeake Bay, 1949–1951." Chesapeake Bay Institute, The Johns Hopkins University, Reference no. 52-4.

Whaley, R. C., *et al.* 1966. "Nutrient Data Summary, 1964, 1965, 1966: Upper Chesapeake Bay (Smith Point to Turkey Point), Potomac, South, Severn, Magothy, Back, Chester, the Miles Rivers, and Eastern Bay." Chesapeake Bay Institute, The Johns Hopkins University, Special Report no. 12, Reference no. 66-4.

Yates, C. C. 1913. *Survey of Oyster Bars of Maryland, 1906–1912*. U.S. Department of Commerce, Coast and Geodetic Survey.

THE JOHNS HOPKINS UNIVERSITY PRESS

This book was composed in Helvetica Light text and Helvetica display type by Typoservice Corporation from a design by Victoria Dudley. It was printed by John D. Lucas Printing Company on Mohawk, 90-lb. Navigation text, smooth finish, and bound by Optic Bindery, Inc. in Holliston Sailcloth.

Library of Congress Cataloging in Publication Data

Lippson, Alice Jane.
    The Chesapeake Bay in Maryland: An atlas of natural resources.

    Bibliography: p.
    1. Aquatic resources—Maryland. 2. Aquatic resources—
Chesapeake Bay. 3. Aquatic resources—Maryland—Maps.
4. Aquatic resources—Chesapeake Bay—Maps. I. Maryland.
University. National Resources Institute. II. Title.
QH105.M3L56   333'.9'50916347   72-12352
ISBN 0-8018-1467-7
ISBN 0-8018-1468-5 (pbk)